# TEACHINGS OF THE TAO

# Teachings

## OF THE

---

*Readings from the
Taoist Spiritual
Tradition*

# TAO

SELECTED AND TRANSLATED BY

*Eva Wong*

SHAMBHALA

Boston & London

1997

B
127
.T3
T43
1997

SHAMBHALA PUBLICATIONS, INC.
Horticultural Hall
300 Massachusetts Avenue
Boston, Massachusetts 02115

9  8  7  6  5  4  3  2  1

*Printed in Canada*

❀ This edition is printed on acid-free paper that meets the
American National Standards Institute z39.48 Standard.

Distributed in the United States by Random House, Inc.,
and in Canada by Random House of Canada Ltd

*Library of Congress Cataloging-in-Publication Data*
Teachings of the Tao: readings from the Taoist spiritual tradition /
selected and translated by Eva Wong.
p.  cm.
ISBN 1-57062-245-0 (alk. paper)
1. Tao.  2. Taoism.  3. Spiritual life—Taoism.  I. Wong, Eva,
1951–
B127.T3T43  1997      96-9728
299'.5144—dc20      CIP

# Contents

Introduction     1

1. The Ways of the Earth and Sky:
   The Shamanic Origins of Taoism     9
   *Ch'u-t'zu* (Songs from the Land of Ch'u)     9

2. The Path of Wu-wei: The Classics
   of Taoism     25
   *Tao-te ching*     25
   *Chuang-tzu*     33
   *Lieh-tzu*     40

3. Honoring the Sacred: Devotional
   Taoism     51
   *T'ai-p'ing ching ch'ao* (Essentials of the
   Classic of Peace and Balance)     52
   *Pei-tou yen-sheng ching* (The North Star
   Scripture of Longevity)     56

4. The Tao Within: Mystical Taoism     66
   *Shang-ch'ing huang-t'ing nei-ching yü-ching*
   (The Yellow Court Jade Classic of the Internal
   Images of the High Pure Realm)     67

*Shang-ch'ing chin-ch'üeh ti-chün wu-tou san-yüan t'u-chüeh* (The Lord of the Golden Tower of the High Pure Realm's Instructions on [Visualizing] the Five Bushels and the Three Ones)    73

5. In Search of Immortality: Taoist Internal Alchemy    78
   *Tsan-tung-chi* (The Triplex Unity)    78
   *Wu-jen p'ien* (Understanding Reality)    87

6. In the Playing Fields of Power: Taoist Magic and Sorcery    95
   Stories of Taoist Immortals, Magicians, and Sorcerers    95
   *Feng-shen yen-yi* (Investiture of the Gods)    104

7. The Tao in Everyday Life: Taoist Ethics    108
   *Chih-sun-tzu chung-ch'ieh ching* (Master Red Pine's Book of Discipline)    108

8. Encountering the Sacred: The Taoist Ceremonies    115
   The Fa-lu (Lighting the Stove) Chants    115
   *Chai-chieh-lu* (Correct Procedures of Purification and Preparation for Festival Services)    121

9. The Arts of Longevity: Cultivating the Mind    126
   *Shang-ch'ing t'ai-shang ti-chün chiu-chen chung-ching* (Scripture of the High Pure

Realm's Highest Celestial Lord's Nine
True Forms) 126
*Tung-hsüan ling-pao ting-kuan ching*
(The Mysterious Grotto Sacred Spirit
Scripture on Concentrated Observation) 131
*Seven Taoist Masters* 135

10. The Arts of Longevity: Cultivating
the Body 138
*Yi-men ch'ang-seng pi-shu* (Chen Hsi-yi's
Secret Methods of Longevity) 138
*Chang San-feng t'ai-chi lien-tan pi-chüeh*
(Chang San-feng's Secret T'ai-chi Method
for Cultivating the Elixir) 148

# Introduction

"THE TAO THAT CAN BE SPOKEN OF IS not the real way. That which can be named is only transient. Run straight into it and you will not see its head. Follow it from behind and you will not see its back." Anyone who writes about Taoism is challenged by these statements from the *Tao-te ching*. However, although the Tao cannot be described by words, words can allow us to catch a fleeting glimpse of that mysterious energy of the universe which is the source of life.

The Taoist spiritual tradition is a vast ocean. Flowing into it are the indigenous beliefs of the early Chinese, the personal vision of the sages, the theories and findings of the natural and medical sciences, and influences from Buddhism and Hinduism. However, despite influences from India and Central Asia, Taoism is deeply rooted in the history and culture of China. It is a tradition that goes back several thousand years to the beginnings of Chinese civilization.

When I was growing up in Hong Kong, I received a Western education at school and a traditional Chinese education at home. I was told by my elders that it was important to know the history and the traditions of my people, and that persons who are not in touch with their tradition are like weeds blown by the wind. To me, it has always been an honor and a privilege to be taught the wisdom of my ancestors. As my understanding of Chinese history and philosophy deepened, I realized that it was in Taoism, not Buddhism or Confucianism, that the sacred and spiritual traditions of China are preserved. Confucianism may have shaped Chinese cultural behavior, but Taoism has shaped the soul and the spirit of the Chinese people.

Before I moved to the United States, I assumed naively that most Chinese were brought up with a sense of their history and their ancestral traditions. But after I settled in the U.S., I found that for many Chinese Americans, tradition only went as far as their grandparents who left China to emigrate to the New World. Now, after several generations of assimilation, many Chinese Americans want to be reconnected with the roots of their culture, especially the sacred and spiritual traditions. As they are unable to read classical Chinese, their only access to the wisdom of their ancestors is through translations. I dedicate this book to them and hope that it will help them in the journey back to their origins.

While living in the U.S., I met many Westerners who wish to experience the Taoist spiritual tradition as participants rather than study it as detached observers. I also dedicate this book to them and hope that it will help them explore and understand the spiritual tradition of a culture which is so different from their own.

The readings in this book are chosen to represent a wide range of Taoist knowledge and wisdom. They are selected from the Taoist canon and post-canon collections unless otherwise stated.

## *The Texts of Taoism and the Taoist Canon*

The Taoist canon is the official collection of the scriptures of Taoism. The current edition of the canon consists of 1,473 volumes of texts. The earliest attempt at categorizing the Taoist texts occurred in the fifth century CE. Lu Hsiu-ching, a Taoist scholar and priest, divided the Taoist texts into seven groups. He named the three major groups of the Taoist scriptures Tung-chen (Cavern of the Realized), Tung-hsüan (Cavern of the Mysterious), and Tung-shen (Cavern of the Spirit), and the four minor sections T'ai-hsüan (Great Mystery), T'ai-p'ing (Great Balance), T'ai-ch'ing (Great Pure), and Cheng-i (Orthodox Classics).

In Lu's system, the Tung-chen section contained the books of the Shang-ch'ing (High Pure) School. These texts first appeared in the Eastern Chin dynasty (317–420 CE). Legend says that the earliest Shang-ch'ing texts were revealed to Yang Hsi by Lady Wei, a Taoist mystic and founder of the Shang-ch'ing movement. The Tung-hsüan section contained the Ling-pao (Sacred Spirit) scriptures. These were collected by Ko Hsüan, a relative of Ko Hung, the distinguished alchemist of the fourth century CE. The Ling-pao texts are a collection of rituals, liturgies, and talismans. The third group, the Tung-shen section, contained the books known as the *San-huang ching* (Scriptures of the Three Lords). They are primarily magical formulae and invocations, and were reputed to have come from the Era of the Three Kingdoms (220–265 CE). During the early T'ang dynasty (ca. seventh century CE), the books of the *San-huang ching* were burned. In later compilations of the canon, their place was taken by *Tao-te ching* and its commentaries.

The T'ai-hsüan texts were reputed to have been transmitted by Lao-tzu to Wen-tzu. They include the *Tao-te ching*, the *Chuang-tzu*, the *Lieh-tzu*, and the *Hsi-hsing ching* (Scripture of Western Ascension). Most of the texts in this section are treatises on stilling the mind, cultivating longevity, and living a simple and unencumbered life. However, a twist of fate in the T'ang dynasty took these books away from the T'ai-hsüan section and placed them in the Tung-chen group. The T'ai-p'ing texts consist of the volumes of a monumental work called the *T'ai-p'ing ching* (Classic of Peace and Balance). When Lu Hsiu-ching compiled his catalog of Taoist books in the fifth century CE, the *T'ai-p'ing ching* was more voluminous than it is now. The question of its authorship is still debated, but it is most likely a text of the Eastern Han dynasty (25–220 CE). It discusses the ideals of a utopian kingdom and contains talismans of healing and deliverance from disasters. The T'ai-ch'ing texts formed the earliest collection of treatises on ingesting minerals and herbs to attain immortality. The movement associated with these techniques of attaining longevity is called the External Pill (*wai-tan*) or External Alchemy school because it advocates the use of external substances in rejuvenating the body. The last entry in Lu Hsiu-ching's catalog of Taoist texts is the *Cheng-i meng-wei lu* (Protocols of the Classic Orthodox Practice). These are the texts of the Celestial Masters sect (*t'ien-shih tao*) founded by Chang Tao-ling in the third century CE.

The next compilation of the books of Taoism occurred during the T'ang dynasty (618–906 CE). The first official edition of the Taoist canon was completed and printed in 748 CE and was named *K'ai-yüan pao-tsang* (The Precious Scriptures Collected in the Reign of Emperor K'ai-yüan). Unfortunately, this edition of the Taoist canon perished in the chaos that surrounded the fall of the T'ang dynasty.

During the Northern Sung dynasty (960–1126 CE), a distinguished Taoist scholar and practitioner named Chang Chün-fang gathered the remnants of the Taoist canon of the T'ang dynasty and collated the texts into the categories first named by Lu Hsiu-ching. Moreover, he selected the best of the Taoist texts and edited them into a Taoist encyclopedia called the *Yun-chi ch'i-ch'ien* (The Seven Bamboo Strips of the Cloud-Hidden Satchel). Not interested in the liturgical form of Taoism, Chang Chün-fang omitted the rituals and ceremonies of the *Cheng-i men-wei* scriptures from his encyclopedia.

The Taoist canon of the Sung dynasty did not survive the violent end of that dynasty. What was left of a vast collection was rescued by the students of Ch'iu Ch'ang-ch'un, one of the Seven Masters of the Complete Reality school, during the Chin dynasty of the Manchus (1115–1234 CE). They edited the texts into the *Yüan-tu tao-tsang* (The Taoist Canon Collected in the Reign of Emperor Yüan-tu). Unfortunately, this canon was destroyed during the Yüan dynasty (1271–1368 CE) in a burning of Taoist texts by militant Buddhists.

It was not until the reign of Emperor Cheng T'ung (1436–1449 CE) in the Ming dynasty (1368–1644 CE) that an edict was issued to compile all the existing Taoist books of the time into a canon. This was the *Cheng-t'ung tao-tsang*, the Taoist canon that we have today.

The *Cheng-t'ung Taoist Canon* was organized around the structure of Lu Hsiu-ching's fifth-century collection. In the Tung-chen section are the scriptures of Shang-ch'ing Taoism and some Ling-pao talismans and ceremonies. Interestingly, Chang Po-tuan's classic of internal alchemy, the *Wu-jen p'ien* (Understanding Reality) and its commentaries are included in this section, as is the *Huang-ti yin-fu ching* (The Yellow Emperor's Classic of Yin Convergence). The Tung-hsüan section consists of mostly Ling-pao scriptures and some Shang-ch'ing texts. However, the Shang-ch'ing classic, *Huang-t'ing nei–ching yü-ching* (The Yellow Court Jade Classic of Internal Images) is placed in this section. We do not know why this important Shang-ch'ing text was placed in a section that contains predominantly Ling-pao texts. The Tung-shen section contains some Ling-pao texts, the most famous of them being the *Pei-tou yen-sheng ching* (North Star Scripture of Longevity). The *Tao-te ching*, the *Chuang-tzu*, and their commentaries are also placed in the Tung-shen section, as are various texts attributed to or were inspired by Lao-tzu.

The T'ai-hsüan section mostly consists of texts of internal alchemy, including the classic *Tsan-tung-chi* (The Triplex Unity). The *Huang-ti nei-ching* (The Yellow Emperor's Classic of the Internals) is also included here. In this section is also the great encyclopedia of Taoist knowledge, the *Yun-chi ch'i-ch'ien* (Seven Bamboo Strips of the Cloud-Hidden Satchel) as well as Shao K'ang-chieh's classic work on divination, the *Wang-chi ching* (Treatise on the Celestial Pathways). Many formulae of the External Pill school, or external alchemy, are also collected here. The T'ai-p'ing section contains primarily the *T'ai-p'ing ching* (Classic of Peace and Balance) and some Ling-pao talismans and ceremonies. Interestingly, the poetry of Wang Ch'ung-yang, one of the greatest proponents of the Complete Reality school of Taoism, is collected here, as are the writings of his disciples, Sun Pu-erh and Ch'iu Ch'ang-ch'un, two of the Seven Taoist Masters. In the T'ai-ch'ing section are writings of philosophers who are generally not classified as Taoists. In this section are the works of Mo-tzu the philosopher of universal love, Sun-tzu the military strategist, Han-fei-tzu the legalist, and Kung-sun Lung the sophist. The classic text of Taoist ethics, the *T'ai-shang kan-ying p'ien* (Lao-tzu's Treatise on the Response of the Tao), is also collected here, as is the encyclopedic work of Ko Hung titled *Pao-p'u-tzu* (The Sage Who Embraces Simplicity). Cheng-i, the last section of the *Cheng-t'ung Taoist Canon*, consists of mostly the scriptures, ceremonies, and talismans of the Cheng-i Meng-wei, or Celestial Teachers' Way of Taoism. For reasons unknown, some Shang-ch'ing scriptures are also included in this section.

A hundred years or so after the *Cheng-t'ung Taoist Canon* was printed, a supplement was added during the reign of the Ming emperor Wan Li (1573–1619 CE). This supplement is known as the *Wan-li Taoist Canon*. Both canons have been preserved to this day. Most of the Taoist books written after the compilation of the Taoist canon in the Ming dynasty have been collected by Hsiao T'ien-shih, a Taoist scholar in Taiwan, and are published in a series of books titled *Tao-tsang ching-hua* (The Essential Texts of Taoism). Needless to say, Hsiao T'ien-shih's collection is not exhaustive, and there are many Taoist texts that are not included in any canon, old or new.

The Taoist canon is distinct from the sacred scriptures of other spiritual traditions in that it is an "open" canon. New texts are being added to it continuously. Perhaps the Taoist canon is open-ended because Taoists are practical people who, being more concerned with the workability of practices than with orthodoxy of theology or philosophy, never entertained the idea of a closed system of knowledge. Or maybe it is because they acknowledged that the Tao cannot be understood by words and conceptual thinking, and therefore human attempts at understanding the Tao would never be complete.

The readings in this book represent approaches to the Tao as well as expressions of Taoist spirituality. In preparing this book, I have tried to let the texts speak for themselves. Other than a brief introduction to each text and occasional translator's notes, there are no commentaries or discussions of the texts. Readers who want more information on the various aspects of Taoism can refer to my book *The Shambhala Guide to Taoism*, where the history, theories, and practices of Taoism are presented in detail.

# 1

## *The Ways of the Earth and Sky*

### THE SHAMANIC ORIGINS OF TAOISM

THE TAOIST SPIRITUAL TRADITION IS rooted in the shamanic beliefs of early China. The giants of Taoist thinking, Lao-tzu and Chuang-tzu, were natives of the feudal state of Ch'u in the Eastern Chou dynasty (770–1221 BCE), where shamanism had a strong influence on the beliefs and cultural practices of the people. The shamanic culture of Ch'u is best illustrated by a collection of poetry titled the *Ch'u-tz'u* (Songs of the Land of Ch'u). The sacredness of nature, the ecstatic union of the shaman and the nature spirits, and the flight to the celestial realm are the themes of these poems. Now, three thousand years later, these themes are still a part of the spiritual tradition of Taoism.

### *The* Ch'u-tz'u *(Songs of the Land of Ch'u)*

The poems of the *Ch'u-tz'u* were either shamanic songs or were inspired by shamanic experiences. Most of the poems were written by Ch'ü Yüan, a native of Ch'u and one of the greatest poets of early China.

In Ch'u culture, nature was sacred. The people's connection with nature was not one of distant respect but of passionate love. The Ch'u shaman's relationship with the spirits of nature was like that of a lover, and the dances and ceremonies were humanity's attempts to "seduce" the sacred powers.

The section in the *Ch'u-tz'u* titled "Nine Songs" best illustrates the shamanic tradition of Ch'u. These songs were sung in the sacred ceremonies that honor the spirits of nature. In the ceremony, one shaman, called the spirit-shaman (*shen-wu*), usually took on the persona of the spirit, and another shaman, who was the leader of the ceremony, played the part of the mortal. Unfortunately, the original text of "Nine Songs" does not indicate which stanzas were sung by which shaman, and this has caused much confusion in understanding the songs and translating them. However, if we listen to the mood and style of the text, it is possible to identify the verses sung by the spirit-shaman and those sung by the leader of the ceremony.

In the translation that follows, I have delineated the parts performed by the singers. I think this brings out the feel of the "Nine Songs" as they were originally performed. As you read these selections, note the usage of plants and herbs in the ceremonies, and the power of music and song in renewing the bond between humanity and the sacred powers.

## *The Nine Songs*

### 1. SONG TO THE GREAT UNITY, LORD OF THE EAST

*Sung by the shaman leading the ceremony*:
It is a beautiful day.
It is an auspicious hour.
We stand silently in awe before the altar of the Great Lord
    on high.
Long swords of jade are in our hands;
Pendants of jade hang from our belts;
Our ornaments jingle as they clash against each other.
Look, the sacred altar is laden with jade and jeweled bowls,
And on it are fragrant flowers and grasses.
We offer meats wrapped in leaves,
And serve them on mats of orchids.
We offer cinnamon wine and sauces of hot peppers.
Together we lift our drumsticks
And begin to beat a rhythm.
Slowly and solemnly we start our singing;
Then, as we hear the pipes and zithers,
Everyone joins in a loud and shrill song.
The sacred shamaness is in her colorful robe;
She begins to dance.
The air is filled with sweet fragrance.
Now the strings play faster;
The five notes are sounding in harmony.
Great One, enjoy and be merry with us.

## 2. SONG TO THE LORD-WITHIN-THE-CLOUDS

*Sung by the shaman leading the ceremony*:
We bathe and wash our hair in water scented with orchid
    leaves;
We put on our robes, decked out like flowers of many
    colors.
The Lord-within-the-Clouds comes down to us,
His sacred light shining with eternal brilliance.
Now he rests in his palace,
Shining together with the sun and moon.
Now he flies his dragon-chariot,
Dressed in majestic splendor.
Now he stays for a while;
Now he flies swiftly and wanders in the sky.
Bright One, you have come to us,
But suddenly you are off again in the clouds.
You look at our lands from high;
Your travels take you over many places.
Where will you go now?
I sigh when I think of you,
And my heart grieves that you cannot be with me.

## 3. SONG TO THE LORD OF THE RIVER

*Sung by the shamaness leading the ceremony*:
You hesitate and do not come to me;
What is it that keeps you from leaving your island?

*Sung by the Lord of the River (spirit-shaman)*:
I am attractive and beautiful;
I come to you in my cinnamon bark canoe.
I glide softly on the waters without a ripple,
For I have asked the waves of the river to be still.

*Sung by the shamaness leading the ceremony*:
I long for you and yet you do not come.
Sadly I play my flute.
Whom do I think of but you?

*Sung by the Lord of the River (spirit-shaman)*:
I fly north on my dragon;
Then I turn toward the Tung-t'ing Lake.
My boat is decorated with care:
The hull is lined with sweet clover;
The sails are made of fig leaves;
The oars are made of iris stems;
And I have orchids for my banners.
Gazing at the sea strand in the distance,
I step across the great river and display my magical powers.

*Sung by the shamaness leading the ceremony*:
You have shown your power and yet you do not come;
My attendants are crying for my sake.
Tears run freely down my cheeks,
And I am sick with longing for you.

With my oars of cinnamon bark and orchid leaves,
I plow my way through ice and snow.
My efforts are like gathering figs in the water,
And plucking lotuses from treetops.
When feelings of love are not deep,
You will easily be separated from me.
Fast as waters running through stony shallows,
You fly away on your dragon.
Faithless love and untrusting friendship
Only cause pain and sorrow.
You broke your promise to me,
And made the excuse that you did not have time.
I race along the banks of the river in the morning;
In the evening I stop to rest at the island in the north.
Birds roost on the roof of the hut;
Water laps on the shores.
I throw my jade ring into the river;
I abandon my jade pendant to the flowing waters;
I gather sweet grass on the fragrant island
And think of giving them to your attendants.
Lost opportunities are hard to recover,
And I can only stay and play a little longer.

## 4. SONG TO THE LADY OF THE RIVER

*Sung by the shaman leading the ceremony*:
The Lady descends to the northern banks.
When I strain my eyes and cannot see her,
My heart breaks with sorrow.

The gentle autumn wind is blowing;
Waves ripple through the waters of Tung-t'ing Lake,
And leaves on the trees are falling.
I climb onto the white tops of the marsh grass
And gaze longingly.
My love and I have agreed to meet here,
And I wait eagerly as the evening light falls.
But why are the birds resting on the duckweeds?
And why are the fishing nets hanging from the trees?
The Yüan River has angelicas of flavoring oil;
The Li River has orchids.
I think of you all the time,
But I am afraid to say it.
Trembling with anticipation, I gaze toward the distance
And listen to the murmur of the waters.
Why are the deer feeding in the courtyards?
Why are dragons lying in shallow water?
In the morning I drive my horses by the river,
In the evening I cross to the western bank.
I hear my love calling my name;
I will follow her chariot to the farthest places.
I have built a hut in the waters
And covered the roof with lotus leaves.
I have decorated the walls with iris;
I have put purple shells in the courtyard
And adorned the hall with fragrant pepper.
The beams are made of cinnamon wood,
And the rafters are made of orchids.
I have hung lintels over the doorway

And decorated our bedchamber with peonies.
I have used sweet clover to make window screens
And have woven together fig leaves for hangings.
I have used white jade to hold down our sleeping mats;
I have scattered stone-orchids to scent the floor;
I have placed white flags over the lotus thatch
And bound them with stalks.
I have planted many fragrant herbs in the courtyard;
And I have scented the gateway with exquisite perfumes.
Even the spirits of Doubting Mountain will come to
    welcome you,
Rushing here like a host of windborne clouds.
I have torn the sleeves off my robe and thrown them into
    the river;
I have taken off my tunic and abandoned it by the swells.
I have plucked sweet grass from the island
To send them to you, who are far away.
Opportunities are hard to come by,
And I can only stay and play a little longer.

## 5. SONG TO THE GREAT LORD OF DESTINY

*Sung by the Great Lord of Destiny (spirit-shaman)*:
Open wide the gates of the sky.
I come riding on the black clouds.
I order the whirlwind to be my herald
And call the rainstorm to wash away the dust.

*Sung by the shaman who is leading the ceremony*:
Great One, you hover and descend to me;

I will climb and follow you
Over the heights of Kong-sang Mountain.

*Sung by the Great Lord of Destiny (spirit-shaman)*:
This world and all its people;
Their lives, long or short, are in my hands.

*Sung by the shaman leading the ceremony*:
Serenely and majestically you soar in the sky;
You ride on the clear vapor of the sky and earth,
And on the breath of yin and yang.
Speedily I will go with you to far-off places,
Leading the lord of the sky to the great mountains.

*Sung by the Great Lord of Destiny (spirit-shaman)*:
My long robes flutter in the wind;
My jade pendants, in brilliant color, dazzle in the light.
Ah, the changes of yin and yang in the universe;
None of the mortals know what I can do.

*Sung by the shaman leading the ceremony*:
I have plucked the jadelike flower of the hemp
To give to the one who is far away.
I am getting old, and if we do not stay together,
I am afraid that we will become strangers.
Driving your dragon-chariot with thundering wheels,
You fly high in the sky.
But here I stand on the ground, holding a stick of
    cinnamon;

My longing for you causing me pain.
What can I do with my sorrow?
I only hope that we will be together forever.
But each life has its destiny.
Meetings or partings, who can decide what will happen?

## 6.  SONG TO THE PROTECTOR OF THE YOUNG ONES

*Sung by the Protector of the Young Ones (spirit-shaman)*:
Autumn orchid and parsley flowers
Grow in rows below my hall.
Green leaves and white flowers
Send their fragrance strongly to me.
People have always wanted children and grandchildren;
Why do you fuss over them?


*Sung by the shamaness leading the ceremony*:
The autumn orchids bloom luxuriantly,
Their leaves green and flowers purple.
The hall is filled with beautiful ladies;
You suddenly turned your seductive gaze to me.
You came without a word,
And you left without goodbye.
Riding on the whirlwind, with clouds as your banners,
You are gone.
No pain is greater than parting with life,
And no greater happiness is there than finding a friend.
Wearing a robe of lotus and a belt of sweet clover,
Swiftly you came, and swiftly you left.

At night you rest near the kingdom of the sky.
Are you waiting for someone at the edge of the clouds?
I long to bathe with you in the celestial pool
And watch you dry your hair in the rising sun.
I keep looking and looking, but you do not come.
What can I do but turn to face the wind
And break into a loud song.
Riding on a chariot covered with peacock feathers,
With banners of brilliant green,
You climb into the nine realms of the sky to touch the stars.
You lift your long sword high to protect your beautiful
    children.
Only you are the true judge of all the people.

## 7. Song to the Lord of the East

*Sung by the Lord of the East (spirit-shaman):*
Slowly I rise from the east,
My light shining on the wooden gate of my house.
Driving my horses slowly forward,
Night gives way to the pale light of dawn.


*Sung by a group of shamans:*
The Sacred One drives his dragon-chariot,
Borne on the breath of thunder;
His banners of clouds fluttering in the wind.
I sigh as I rise to the sky above;
My heart is hesitant, and I do not wish to leave my home
    below.

Your colors at dawn are so enticing.
All who see you are intoxicated and forget to return home.
We tighten the strings of our zithers
And beat our drums together;
We strike the bells and shake the bell-stand;
And we play our pipes and flutes.
We are beautiful and virtuous;
We whirl around, sometimes slow and sometimes fast.
As we sing, everyone breaks into a dance
To the notes of the music and the beat of the rhythm.
The Sacred One has come.
Your many spirit attendants will darken your light.


*Sung by the Lord of the East (spirit-shaman)*:
I dress myself in a shirt of blue and a skirt of white
And soar into the sky.
I aim my long arrow and shoot at the Sky Wolf.
Grasping my bow, I descend back to earth.
I lift the handle of the Dipper to ladle cinnamon wine;
Holding the reins of my horses, I urge them across the sky;
And in the darkness of night I make my journey back to the
    east.


## 8. SONG TO THE EARL OF THE RIVER

*Sung by shaman leading the ceremony*:
I travel with you to play in the nine rivers.
The gusty winds whip up the breakers.
We ride on a water-chariot with lotus leaves as canopy.

Two dragons draw the chariot,
And two serpents accompany us at our side.
We climb to the top of the Kun-lun Mountains,
And look in the four directions.
My heart flutters and leaps in ecstasy.
The sky will darken soon;
But wanting to stay longer,
I forget about going home.
I gaze at the distant shores,
And my heart is filled with longing.
Your chamber is made of fish scales and your hall of dragon
     skin;
You have filled your palace with pearls and purple shells.
Why do you have to live in the water,
And travel on the backs of great turtles to catch brightly
     striped fish?
Come with me instead to play on the sandy islands.
We'll roll around with the floods that come our way.
You and I shake hands goodbye as you continue east.
Let me accompany you as far as the southern bank.
The waves swell up to welcome you,
While shoals of fishes accompany me back home.

## 9. SONG TO THE MOUNTAIN SPIRIT

*Sung by a group of shamans*:
There appears to be someone deep in the mountains,
Wearing a cloak of fig leaves and a belt of rabbit fur.
You look at me with penetrating eyes and a friendly smile.

Lady, I know you desire my good looks.
You are driving two leopards and leading two striped lynxes.
Your chariot is made of magnolia,
And your banners are woven with cinnamon sticks.
You are dressed in a cloak of stone-orchids;
The folds are gathered neatly with a belt of stalks.
You pluck sweet grass to give to the one you love.
Here I am in the dense bamboo forest;
The trees are so thick that I can't even see the sky.
The mountain trails are dangerous;
That is why I am late.
Alone, I stand on top of the mountain;
The dense clouds floating down below.
The east wind comes in;
The rains will be here soon.
I am so happy to be with you that
I forget about going home.
I am getting old;
What chances will be left for me to feel the goodness of
    life?
Alone, I gather mushrooms in the mountains.
I can only see the scattered rocks
And arrowroots creeping through them.
Are you thinking of me although you do not have the time
    to come?
I long for you, and in sorrow I forget that I have to go.
Wanderer in the mountains, you are like the sweet grass;
You drink from the rock spring
And rest beneath the pine and fir.

Are you really thinking of me?
I cannot be certain.
The thunder rumbles;
The rain darkens the sky;
Monkeys and apes scream mournful cries;
The wind moans loudly and the leaves whistle.
I think of you, and my heart is filled with sadness.

**NOTES ON THE TRANSLATION**

I have titled song number 3 "Song to the Lord of the River"
and number 4 "Song to the Lady of the River." I disagree
with David Hawkes's interpretation (in the *Ch'u-tz'u: Songs
of the South*) that song number 3 is addressed to a goddess.
The deity in question here is the Shang-chün. *Chün* is tra-
ditionally a respected title for a male. It can be translated
as "gentleman" or "husband," and it is typically not used to
address a female. Songs number 3 and 4 also form a pair.
The chief singer of the Song to the Lord of the River is a
shamaness; it is she who longs for her beloved, the male
river spirit. On the other hand, the chief singer of the Song
to the Lady of the River is a shaman, and he is longing for
his lover, the female river spirit.

I have titled song number 6 "Song to the Protector of the
Young Ones." I also disagree with Hawkes's interpretation
that this song addresses a "lesser" lord of destiny and that
some lines do not belong here. The word *hsiao* can mean
"young" or "less." The other two words, *ssu-ming*, can either
mean "giver of life" or "controller of destiny." When inter-

preted as "giver of life to the young ones," the spirit invoked in the song is not a controller of destiny who has lesser powers than the one in song number 5, but is a totally different kind of power: one who grants life to the young ones. Read this way, the entire poem forms a cohesive unit and no lines are out of place. Personally, I think this rendering is more consistent with Ch'u culture. Children were a blessing, and fertility was much desired among the southern tribes. Unlike the desolate north, the southern lands could support its population, and a family with many children was considered a "rich" family. Thus, I feel that the Song to the Protector of the Young Ones is better understood as a song asking the sacred power to grant fertility.

Many songs describe various species of plants used in the shamanic dance. In the translation I have reduced the use of botanical names and have used common plant names that the general reader is more familiar with.

# 2

## The Path of Wu-wei

### THE CLASSICS OF TAOISM

THE *LAO-TZU (TAO-TE CHING), CHUANG-tzu*, and *Lieh-tzu* are called the Three Classics of Taoism. Although they were written over two thousand years ago, their wisdom is timeless, and their teachings are remarkably relevant to our times. I have chosen sections from these three books to highlight three major themes in the teachings of Taoism: the nature of the Tao, sagehood, and cultivating life. All three books address similar issues, but they speak differently, as if each has a character and life of its own. The *Lao-tzu*, or *Tao-te ching*, is poetic in style and serious in its approach. The *Chuang-tzu* is prose and is wild and idiosyncratic. The *Lieh-tzu* tells stories and is humorous. Serious wisdom, crazy wisdom, and humorous wisdom, these books contain some of the best philosophy and literature that the Chinese culture has ever produced.

### Tao-te ching

The *Tao-te ching* was originally titled *Lao-tzu*. Although it was named *Tao-te ching* by Taoist scholar Wang Pi (226–

249 CE), who felt that the book dealt with the nature of the Tao and the matter of virtue (*te*), the *Lao-tzu* did not receive that official title until the reign of Emperor Hsüan Tsung (739–782 CE) in the T'ang dynasty.

Who wrote the *Tao-te ching*? There are several theories. Some scholars maintain that the book was written by several people, one of whom was indeed a historical person named Li Erh, now known as Lao-tzu. Other parts of the book were written either by students of Lao-tzu or by thinkers who were sympathetic to his teachings. Others say that Lao-tzu the person was a fictitious character and that the book represents the teachings of a loosely knit group of thinkers who held similar ideas. When the book was put together, it was titled *Lao-tzu* because it contained the "teachings of the old wise ones" (*lao* means "old," and *tzu* means "wise one"). There is, however, a general agreement that the book was the work of more than one person.

Most people agree that the *Tao-te ching* was written over a period of time, but there is no consensus as to when. Some date it to the Spring and Autumn Period (770–476 BCE) of the Eastern Chou dynasty (770–221 BCE), placing the historical Lao-tzu as a contemporary of Confucius. Others argue that because its style differs from the Confucian classics like the *Analects*, it could not have been written during the time of Confucius. Personally, I agree with the earlier dating for several reasons. First, Ssu-ma Ch'ien, the Grand Historian, noted that Lao-tzu was a native of Ch'u who lived in the time of Confucius and that the two men had met and discussed matters of ceremonies and rituals. I find this believable since Confucius was interested in the ancient rituals and collected them in the *Li-chi* (Book of Rites), and Lao-tzu was a librarian of the imperial archives. Thus, it is likely that Confucius could have approached Lao-tzu and consulted him on matters of rituals and rites. Second, just because the *Tao-te ching* and the Confucian classics differ in style does not mean that the two works could not be contemporary, especially if we consider the *Tao-te ching* to be a work of a southern culture of Ch'u and the *Analects* to be a work from the northern states of Ch'i and Lu. (Ch'u, Ch'i, and Lu were feudal states of the Eastern Chou dynasty.) In fact, recent Chinese scholars have pointed to the similarity of style between the *Tao-te ching* and the *Ch'u-tz'u*. Thus, it is reasonable that some parts of the *Tao-te ching* could have been written as early as the sixth century BCE, with subsequent additions dating as late as the fourth century BCE. But regardless of who wrote it and when it was written, the *Tao-te ching* is one of the most important classics of Taoism. Its teachings are timeless, and its wisdom transcends culture and history.

The translations that follow are made from the Standard Text found in the Taoist canon.

## *From the* Tao-te Ching

### ON THE TAO

1

The Tao that can be spoken of is not the real way.
That which can be named is only transient.

The nameless was there before the sky and the earth were
    born.
The named is the mother of the ten thousand things.
In nothingness you will see its wonders;
In things you will see its boundaries.
These two come from the same origin, although they have
    different names.
They emerged from somewhere deep and mysterious.
This deep and mysterious place
Is the gateway to all wonders.


4

The Tao is empty.
However, if you use it, it can never be exhausted.
Deep and bottomless,
It may be the ancestor of all things.
It blunts what is sharp,
Unties what is tangled,
Softens what is dazzling,
And merges with the dust.
Deep and hidden,
It appears to last forever.
I do not know whose son it is;
Looks like it was here before the rulers of the sky existed.


14

Try to look at it and you will not see it;
Therefore we call it "unfathomable."
Try to listen to it and you will not hear it;

Therefore we call it "rare."
Try to touch it and you will not feel it;
Therefore we call it "ungraspable."
These three cannot be penetrated further,
For they cannot be separated.
Up high it is not bright;
Down below it is not dark.
Infinite and limitless, we cannot name it,
Because it always reverts to nothingness.
A shape without a shape,
A form without an object,
It is elusive and fleeting.
Run straight into it and you will not see its head;
Follow it from behind and you will not see its back.
Use the way of the ancients to master the situations of the
    present.
To know the origin of the universe
Is to understand the structure of the Tao.


25

There was something undifferentiated but complete.
Born before sky and earth,
Soundless and formless,
It stands on its own ground and is unchanging.
It moves like a circle and never stops.
It can be the mother of the universe.
I do not know its name,
So I call it the Tao.

If forced to name it, I'll call it Great.
It is great because it moves through everything.
It reaches far, yet it returns to where it started.
Therefore the Tao is great;
The sky is great;
Earth is great;
And the ruler of humanity is also great.
There are four great things in world, and the ruler of
    humanity is one of them.
Humanity follows the way of earth;
Earth follows the way of the sky;
The sky follows the way of the Tao;
And the Tao follows its own natural way.


### 34

The Great Tao flows everywhere.
Its course can go left or right.
The ten thousand things depend on it for growth,
And it does not refuse them.
It accomplishes its work and does not claim credit.
It clothes and feeds all things but does not control them.
Always without desire, it can be called small.
The ten thousand things come under its embrace,
But it does not dominate them.
Therefore it can be called great.
Because it does not consider itself as great,
It can accomplish that which is great.

## On Sagehood and Cultivating Life

### 10

Can you unite your spirit with the One and not let it leave?
In concentrating on your breath, can you make it soft like
an infant's?
Can you purify your thoughts and clarify your mind
So that they are spotless?
Can you love your country and people without effort?
In opening and closing the celestial gate,
Can you become the female?
In understanding everything in the universe,
Can you do it without using knowledge?
Give birth to them and nourish them,
But do not possess them.
Help them know that they are not dependent on you.
Guide them but do not control them
This is the most profound virtue.

### 12

The five colors can confuse your sight.
The five sounds can dull your hearing.
The five flavors can injure your sense of taste.
Racing and hunting can drive you mad.
Material goods that are hard to get will hinder your
movement.
Therefore enlightened people care about their stomach and
not their senses.
They discard one and take the other.

### 44

Fame or your body, which do you want more?
Your body or your wealth, which do you value more?
Gain or loss, which do you want more?
If you have a lot of desire, you will probably be extravagant.
The more you hoard, the more you will lose.
Know contentment and you will not be disgraced;
Know when to stop, and you will not meet with danger.
In this way, you will be around for a long time.

### 52

There was a beginning of the world
That may be regarded as the mother of the world.
Attain the mother, and you will know her children.
Hold on to the mother, and you will not meet with harm all
    your life.
Block the openings;
Close the doors;
And all your life you won't have to toil.
·Open the holes,
Meddle in the worldly affairs,
And all your life you will not be saved.
To be able to discern the small is clarity;
To be able to hold on to the soft is strength.
Use the light
To return to brightness.
In this way, you will not invite harm.
This is called practicing that which is permanent.

55

One who embraces virtue fully
Is like an infant.
Poisonous snakes and insects will not sting him;
Fierce beasts will not claw him;
Birds of prey will not strike him.
His bones are weak, his tendons are soft,
But his grasp is strong.
He does not know the union of male and female,
And yet his organ is aroused.
This is because his procreative energy is at its height.
He can cry all day without getting hoarse.
This is because he is in perfect harmony.
To know harmony is to be at one with the permanent;
To know the permanent is to be clear.
To be greedy of life is a sign of misfortune.
If you direct your breath with your mind you will be forcing
    things.
When things reach their prime, they will begin to get old.
This is not the Tao.
What is not the Tao will meet with an early end.

### Chuang-tzu

The *Chuang-tzu* is a collection of essays in thirty-three chapters divided into three sections: the Inner Chapters (*nei-p'ien*), the Outer Chapters (*wai-p'ien*), and the Miscellaneous Chapters (*tsa-p'ien*). Like many ancient texts, the *Chuang-tzu* that we have today is incomplete. The current

*Chuang-tzu* was probably put together in the early fourth century CE. During the T'ang dynasty, the *Chuang-tzu's* status was elevated when it became one of the three Classics of Taoism, together with the *Tao-te ching* and the *Lieh-tzu*.

The writings in the *Chuang-tzu* span over four hundred years of thought, from the fourth century BCE in the Warring States Period (475–221 BCE) of Eastern Chou to the third century CE in the Eastern Han. It is now believed that the Inner Chapters, written between 250 and 300 BCE, are the oldest sections of the book. These chapters were probably written by one person, most likely Chuang-tzu himself. Parts of the Outer Chapters and Miscellaneous Chapters are essays written by various authors sometime between 221 and 25 BCE, during the Ch'in and Han dynasties. Other parts could have been written as late as the Wei and Chin dynasties (between 220–420 CE). Some of the authors were students of Chuang-tzu, while others were Taoist philosophers who lived several hundred years after his time.

The first excerpt is from chapter 2 of the Inner Chapters. The second excerpt, chapter 15, is from the Outer Chapters.

## *On the Tao*

From the *Chuang-tzu*, chapter 2: Discussion on All Things Being Equal

Tzu-ch'i of the southern suburb sat leaning on a table and looked up at the sky. His breathing was slow, as if his mind had wandered off somewhere.

Yen-ch'eng Tzu-yu, who was standing by his side, asked, "What's going on? Can the body become like a withering tree and the wind be like dead ashes? Can the man who sits leaning on the table today be different from the one who sat in the same place yesterday?"

Tzu-ch'i replied, "Yen, you've asked a good question. Today my spirit left my body. Do you understand that? You've heard voices of people, but you haven't heard the voices of the earth. And if you've heard the voices of the earth, you haven't heard the voices of the sky!"

Tzu-yu said, "What does this mean?"

Tzu-ch'i then said, "The Great Earth blows out a vapor and it is called wind. If it doesn't blow, nothing happens. However, when it does, the ten thousand hollows and holes will howl wildly. Haven't you heard their persistent cries? In the high mountains and low hills are deep forests. In these forests are trees whose trunks are so wide that a hundred men can circle them. These trees have openings like noses, mouths, ears, jugs, cups, grain mortars, deep pools, and shallow ponds. When the wind blows, they roar like waves and whistle like arrows shot from bows. Some scream, some make sounds like heavy breathing, some cry, some wail, some laugh, and some sigh. Those in the lead lightly let out an "eeee" and those following behind echo loudly with "yuu." If the wind is gentle, the harmony is faint, but in a strong gale the chorus is deafening. When the wind stops, all the hollows are empty and silent again. Haven't you seen that kind of tossing and swaying going on in the forests?"

Tzu-yu said, "Oh, so the voices of earth are the sounds from the hollows, and the sounds of people are those coming from flutes and pipes. Then, may I ask, what are the voices of the sky?"

Tzu-ch'i replied, "Blowing into the hollows of the ten thousand myriad things in different ways, so that each of them can make its own sound and takes what it needs— this is voice of the sky. But who is directing them to make these sounds?"

Great understanding is broad, and lesser understanding is picky. Great words carry strength and little words are petty and quarrelsome. When people go to sleep, their spirits wander off. When they awake, their bodies are uncomfortable. This is because they get tangled up with everything they contact. Every day they use their minds to scheme. Some brag about themselves, some set up traps for others, and some hide their malicious intentions. Their small fears make them edgy and suspicious. Their big fears make them lose their minds. Some shoot off their arguments like arrows and delight in bickering over right and wrong. Others hold on to their opinions tightly, certain that they are correct. Thus, they fade and die like autumn and winter, decaying day by day. They are so stuck in their condition that it will be hard to get them to turn back. They are so blocked up that not even one whiff of air can come out. Old and withering, their minds are near death, and nothing can restore them to life.

Rapture, anger, sadness, happiness, worry, regret, rashness, stubbornness, modesty, carelessness, bluntness, and pretense are music from empty hollows, bursting out like mushrooms from the damp ground. Day and night they replace each other, springing up in front of us, and we don't even know where they come from!

Let them be, let them be! They're with us morning and evening. We can't exist without them, and they have nothing to latch on to without us. It is the way things are. I don't know how they came about. If they have a true master, then I have not seen it. I can see the actions, but I cannot discern the form. This is because it exists and yet it has no form.

The hundred joints, the nine openings, the six organs all come with my body. Which part do I value most? You say that I should favor all of them. Or is there one that I should like most? Are they all merely servants? If so, then why do they behave in so orderly a fashion? Do they take turns playing ruler and subject? Is there a true lord among them? But whether I know who it is or not, it should not affect the truth of the matter.

## On Sagehood and Cultivating Life

From the *Chuang-tzu*, Chapter 15: Constraining the Will

So it is said, the life of the sage follows the celestial way, and in death he dissolves and merges with all things. In stillness he is at one with the virtue of yin; in movement he flows with yang. He does not bring fortune and does not cause misfortune. He only responds when external circumstances call for it. He only acts when pushed. He only rises up when there is no other alternative. He throws away the whys and wherefores, and follows the celestial way. Therefore, he does not meet with disaster. Nor is he burdened by material things. He is not slandered by people nor punished by the spirits. He floats with life and rests with death. He does not worry and does not scheme. He is like light that does not dazzle. Completely trustworthy, he does not need to make promises. His sleep is dreamless and his waking hours are free from worry. His spirit is pure and his soul is not tired. In emptiness, nothingness, and simplicity, he is in harmony with the celestial way.

Therefore, it is said that grief and happiness pervert virtue, joy and anger obstruct the Tao, and delight and repulsion work against virtue. When the mind is without worry or joy, virtue is complete. When it is at one and unchanging, stillness is complete. When it does not oppose anything, emptiness is complete. When it does not interact with things, simplicity is complete. When it does not resent things, purity is complete.

Thus, it is said that if the body works too hard and does not rest, it will weaken. If the generative energy is used without restraint, it will be exhausted. If it is exhausted, you will be tired. It is the nature of water that if it is not mixed with other things, it will remain clear. If it is not stirred, it will remain still. Dam it and it will not flow. If it stops flowing, it will no longer be clear. Such is the nature of the celestial way. So it is said, be pure and simple and do not be mixed up. To be still, unified, and unchanging, to be simple and nonintrusive, moving with the celestial path—this is the way of cultivating the spirit.

### NOTES ON THE TRANSLATION

Although Burton Watson's translation of the *Chuang-tzu* is considered the standard reference, I have translated some words and phrases differently. My choice of words is based on suggestions made by commentators of the *Chuang-tzu*. In "Discussion on All Things Being Equal," I have used the phrase "my spirit left my body" instead of "I lost myself" (Watson's version) to translate the three Chinese words that are literally "I," "lost," and "me." In the language of Taoism of the time, "I" and "me" in the phrase do not refer to the same subject. "I" refers to mind or spirit, and "me" refers to the body. Thus, I think that the entire phrase may be better rendered as "my spirit left my body." This is more consistent with some Chinese commentaries that suggest that Tzu-ch'i was describing a meditative or trancelike state.

I have also translated the word *yang* as "life" instead of "light." In a Taoist text, *yang* is better rendered as "life," especially in a context where Chuang-tzu was talking about caring for health and sanity in troubled times.

## Lieh-tzu: A Taoist Guide to Practical Living

The *Lieh-tzu* is a collection of stories and philosophical musings. It contains materials written over a period of six hundred years (between 300 BCE and 300 CE). There were twenty sections in the original collection, and these were condensed into the eight sections we have today.

During the hundred years or so after it was compiled, the *Lieh-tzu* did not receive the kind of attention that was given to the *Tao-te ching* and the *Chuang-tzu*. Most scholars believed that its teachings were similar to those of the *Chuang-tzu*, which was sufficient for gaining an understanding of Taoism of the Warring States and early Han periods. If not for the efforts of a scholar of the Eastern Chin (317–420 CE) who edited and wrote a commentary on it, the *Lieh-tzu* probably would have disappeared into oblivion.

Although the *Lieh-tzu* was written by more than one person and the text that we have today is incomplete, it contains some of the best presentations of the teachings of Taoism. Its down-to-earth, humorous, and amusing discussion of the Tao, human nature, and issues that are remarkably relevant to our times make it one of the most accessible Taoist texts ever written.

The following excerpts are from my book *Lieh-tzu: A Taoist Guide to Practical Living*. In this book I attempted to present the teachings of the *Lieh-tzu* by bringing out the "intention" or "voice" of the text. While books are meant to be read, voices are meant to be listened to. In the *Lieh-tzu* I tried to let the text speak as if the philosopher were talking directly to the reader. It is not a translation in the strict sense because I have elaborated on some parts and amalgamated others. Some hard-to-pronounce Chinese names have been omitted to facilitate the continuity of listening to the text. I hope that this method of presenting the *Lieh-tzu* conveys the feel of listening to one of the greatest teachers of Taoism.

## On the Tao

From the *Lieh-tzu*, Part One: The Gifts of Heaven

### THAT WHICH IS NOT BORN GIVES BIRTH TO EVERYTHING

Lieh-tzu was a humble and sincere person. His thoughts and actions tell us he was "uncommonly common." He was unassuming and never displayed his learning. He lived a simple and quiet life and did not compete with others for recognition. Therefore, although he had lived in the kingdom of Cheng for forty years, people in positions of power saw him only as a common citizen. Throughout his life, Lieh-tzu never made a name for himself.

Without the burdens and problems associated with fame and fortune, Lieh-tzu could live leisurely and be free to do what he liked and go where he wanted. To Lieh-tzu, being an unknown citizen was better than being a person of power and responsibility. In a time when politicians played games of intrigue, Lieh-tzu felt it was better to remain silent and be truthful to oneself.

Of course, there are certain things that even a wise sage cannot escape. But, not being bound by custom and social convention, Lieh-tzu was able to deal with adversity much better than anyone else. One year, a famine occurred in Cheng, and Lieh-tzu decided to move to the kingdom of Wei to see if he could make a living there. Moreover, he thought this would give him an opportunity to travel to an unknown country and broaden his learning.

While Lieh-tzu was preparing to leave, a group of his students came to him. They were worried that their teacher might leave them for a long time. They knew Lieh-tzu did not follow any routine, and, if the mood suited him, he might wander for months or years before returning. Therefore, they wanted their teacher to give them some words of wisdom before he departed.

Lieh-tzu was not a person given to casual chatting. After his students begged him tirelessly for half a day, he finally said, "Think about this. Old man sky never says a word, but we can see that everything has its place in the universe. Nature has a lot to teach us. All you need is to open your eyes and look. The changes you see in nature follow a course. The four seasons behave in a regulated way. In truth, all human matters follow the same principles as the workings of the sky and earth. What more is there for me to say?"

His students were not satisfied and continued to pester him with questions. One student said, "Sir, even if you feel there is nothing for you to say, you can at least tell us what your teacher Hu-tzu taught you." Lieh-tzu was silent for a while. Then he smiled and said, "Actually, my teacher Hu-tzu did not say much. He told us to let everything go according to its natural way. However, I did remember a few things he mentioned to some of my fellow students. I'll share them with you now."

Here is what Master Hu-tzu taught:

There are many things in the universe that we don't understand. For example, some plants and animals require help from others to grow and survive, while others don't. We humans rely on plants and animals for food. We also need some of our community to farm the land and raise the livestock to sustain the rest of us. On the other hand, cacti can grow in the most hostile conditions and they do not need much support to survive. In general, those that are less dependent on the external environment for support will find it easier to survive than those that do. They will not die when their supporting environment disappears.

However, we should not look down on those who need to depend on others for survival. We should let them grow naturally in their own way, for their mode of living has its place in maintaining the balance of the universe. If we tried to change their way of life, we would upset the balance of things, and the order of the universe would be disturbed.

All things have their place in the universe, whether it is active or passive, moving or not moving. They fulfill their function in the world simply by being what they are. Everything plays a part in the process of creating, nourishing, transforming, and destroying. The creation of one thing is the destruction of another, and the destruction of one thing is the creation of another. In this way, life carries on in the universe. In every moment there is birth and death and there is coming and going. This process never stops. . . .

If we understand that birth and death are part of the natural order of things, we will know that our lives cannot be controlled by our own efforts, and coming and going are not our own doing. At birth, we take a shape and form; in growth, we undergo development and change; and when our course has run out, we dissolve and return to where we were before we were born.

If we know the order of things, we will understand that when intelligence and wisdom have reached their zenith, they will begin to fade and decay. The rise and fall of shapes, colors, thoughts, and feelings are not subject to control. Because we don't know whence they come or where they go, we can only say that everything that is born comes from the not-born.

From *Lieh-tzu*, Part Six: Effort and Destiny

EFFORT ARGUES WITH DESTINY

One day Effort said to Destiny, "My achievements are greater than yours."

Destiny did not agree. He challenged Effort immediately. "What have you done to make your achievements surpass mine?"

Effort said, "Whether someone lives long or dies young, is rich or poor, will succeed or fail depends on me."

Destiny said at once, "Old P'eng's intelligence did not match the emperors Yao's and Shun's, but he lived a long and healthy life. On the other hand, Yen-hui, Confucius's best student, died when he was eighteen. Confucius's virtue far surpassed the feudal lords', but compared to them he was destitute and poor. The emperor Shang-t'sou was cruel and immoral but lived a prosperous and long life. On the other hand, his ministers who were virtuous met with violent deaths. There was a man who sacrificed his own fortune to allow his brother a chance to be employed by the lord of Cheng. He remained poor and unknown for the rest of his life. Then there was another man who had neither virtue nor ability who became the lord of Ch'i. How about Po-yi and Shu-ch'i, who starved to death in the mountains because they would not compromise their integrity and honor to serve an enemy lord? What can you say about corrupt officials who are rich, or honest, hard-working people who are poor?"

Effort had not expected this barrage of evidence against his assertion. He frowned, but Destiny continued, "If you are as effective as you say, then why don't you make the hard-working people rich? Why don't you give virtuous people a long and prosperous life? Why are the intelligent and able people not employed, and why do stupid people occupy important places in government?"

Effort had no more to say in the face of these challenges, so sheepishly he said to Destiny, "You are right. I do not have much effect after all. But I daresay a lot of things happen the way they do because you've been up to mischief, twisting people's destiny around and enjoying it!"

Destiny then said, "I cannot force the directions of things. I merely open doors for them to go through. If something is going straight, I let it follow the straight path; if something takes a turn I do not hinder it. No one, not you or I, can direct the path of things. Long life or short, rich or poor, success or failure, fortune or misfortune, all come about by themselves. How can I direct events or even know where things would end up?"

## On Sagehood and Cultivating Life

From *Lieh-tzu*, Part Two: The Yellow Emperor

### RIDING ON THE WIND, FLOATING WITH THE CLOUDS

Lieh-tzu had the immortal Old Shang for a teacher and the sage Pai-kao-tzu as a friend. After he had finished his training, he came home riding on the wind and floating on the clouds.

A man named Yin-sheng heard about Lieh-tzu's feat and wanted to learn this skill of riding on the wind. So he went to Lieh-tzu and asked to be his student. So intent was Yin-sheng on learning this skill that he stayed at Lieh-tzu's home and kept pestering the teacher with questions. This went on for several months, but Lieh-tzu only ignored him.

Yin-sheng began to get impatient and then angry that Lieh-tzu was not teaching him. One day, he left in a huff.

When Yin-sheng got home, he calmed down and realized he had been stupid and impulsive, so he went to Lieh-tzu and asked to be his student again. Lieh-tzu simply said, "Why did you come and then leave and then return?"

Yin-sheng said, "When I first came to ask you to teach me, you ignored me. So I got annoyed and left. Then I realized I was too impatient and reckless, so I came back to ask you to accept me as a student again."

Lieh-tzu said, "I had thought you were intelligent, but now I can see you are quite stupid. Listen to what I went through when I learned from my teachers."

Lieh-tzu said:

"When I asked Old Shang to be my master and Pai-kao-tzu to be my friend, I decided to work hard to discipline my body and mind. After three years, I was afraid to have notions of right and wrong and I did not dare to speak words that might offend or please. It was only then that my master glanced at me and acknowledged my presence. Five years later, I thought freely of right and wrong, and spoke freely of approval or disapproval. My master gave me a smile. Seven years later, my thoughts came naturally without any conceptions of right and wrong, and words came naturally without any intention of pleasing or offending. For the first time, my master invited me to sit by his side. Nine years later, no matter what came to my mind or what came out of my mouth, there was nothing that was right or wrong, pleasing or offending. I did not even entertain the idea that Old Shang was my master and Pai-kao-tzu was my friend.

"It was then I became aware that there was no barrier between what was inside and what was outside. My body was illuminated by a bright light. I heard with my eyes and saw with my ears. I used my nose as mouth and my mouth as nose. I experienced the world with the totality of my senses as my spirit gathered and my form dissolved. There was no distinction between muscles and bones. My body stopped being heavy and I felt like a floating leaf. Without knowing it, I was being carried by the wind. Drifting here and there, I did not know whether I rode on the wind or the wind rode on me."

He then looked at Yin-sheng and said, "You had only been here for less than an hour and you got dissatisfied that you were not taught. Look at your condition. The parts of your body do not cooperate; the vapors of the sky and earth do not enter your body; your joints and bones are so heavy that you can't even move. And you want to learn how to ride on the wind?"

When Yin-sheng heard these words he was ashamed and did not ask again about riding on the wind.

From *Lieh-tzu*, Part Seven: Yang-chu

LIFE—TEMPORARILY STAYING IN THE WORLD; DEATH—TEMPORARILY LEAVING

Yang-chu said:
"If you live to be a hundred, it is considered a long life.

However, only one in a thousand persons is that lucky. But if we take a person who has lived a hundred years and look at the time he has spent in his life, we will realize that a hundred years is not a long life. Out of these years, childhood and old age take up at least half the time. In addition, half the day he is asleep. Not to mention the hours during the day that he has idled away. What does that leave him? Moreover, if you take out the times when he is ill, sad, confused, suffering, and not feeling good, there isn't much time left that he can enjoy or be free.

"Some people think they can find satisfaction in good food, fine clothes, lively music, and sexual pleasure. However, when they have all these things, they are not satisfied. They realize happiness is not simply having their material needs met. Thus, society has set up a system of rewards that go beyond material goods. These include titles, social recognition, status, and political power, all wrapped up in a package called self-fulfillment. Attracted by these prizes and goaded on by social pressure, people spend their short lives tiring body and mind to chase after these goals. Perhaps this gives them the feeling that they have achieved something in their lives, but in reality they have sacrificed a lot in life. They can no longer see, hear, act, feel, or think from their hearts. Everything they do is dictated by whether it can get them social gains. In the end, they've spent their lives following other people's demands and never lived a life of their own. How different is this from the life of a slave or a prisoner?

"The ancients understood that life is only a temporary sojourn in this world, and death is a temporary leave. In our short time here, we should listen to our own voices and follow our own hearts. Why not be free and live your own life? Why follow other people's rules and live to please others? When something enjoyable comes your way, you should enjoy it fully. Don't be imprisoned by name or title, for social conventions can lead you away from the natural order of things. It doesn't matter whether you will be remembered in generations ahead, because you will not be there to see it.

"Why spend your life letting other people manipulate you just to get a name and reputation? Why not let your life be guided by your own heart and live without the burdens of fame and recognition?"

# 3

## *Honoring the Sacred Powers*

### DEVOTIONAL TAOISM

THE TAO IS THE SOURCE OF LIFE OF ALL things, and this sacred power is sometimes manifested as deities and spirits. In the Taoist spiritual tradition, devotion is a way of honoring the sacred power that gave us life and nourished us. Also, through devotion, a bond is created between humanity and the sacred, and as long as this bond is maintained, there will be peace and harmony in the universe.

The readings in this chapter are from two of the most famous texts of Taoist devotional literature: the *T'ai-p'ing ching ch'ao* (Essentials of the Classic of Peace and Balance) and the *Pei-tou yen-sheng ching* (The North Star Scripture of Longevity). The excerpt from the *T'ai-p'ing ching ch'ao* gives us a glimpse of how Lao-tzu is portrayed as the chief deity of the Taoist religion. The *Pei-tou yen-sheng ching* is a liturgy that honors the celestial deities of the Northern Bushel Stars (the Big Dipper), who are the rulers of health, longevity, and human destiny.

## T'ai-p'ing ching ch'ao *(Essentials of the Classic of Peace and Balance)*

The *T'ai-p'ing ching ch'ao* consists of excerpts from the *T'ai-p'ing ching*, the book from the Eastern Han dynasty (25–220 CE) that launched the movement of devotional Taoism. Much of the original *T'ai-p'ing ching* is lost, and the version collected in the Taoist canon today is only a small fraction of the original work. The *T'ai-p'ing ching ch'ao* was compiled by a Taoist of the T'ang dynasty. The editor took what he thought were the best parts of the *T'ai-p'ing ching* and compiled them into one book. It is in the *T'ai-p'ing ching ch'ao* that several missing sections of the *T'ai-p'ing ching* are preserved. The story of the birth of Lao-tzu and his deification (translated below) would have been lost if the editor of the *T'ai-p'ing ching ch'ao* had not included it in his book.

## *The Birth of Lao-tzu*

From *T'ai-p'ing ching ch'ao*, Chapter 1

The Great Lord of Longevity is named the Great Balance of the One True Wonderful Vapor, the Latter Sacred Lord of the Nine Mysteries of the High Pure Golden Tower of Heaven. His name is Li and he is descended from the Great High One. He is the fetus of the Great Void of the Jade Emperor. During the time of the Lord of the Great

Mystery and Completeness, in the fifteenth year of the reign of the Great Emperor, when *ping-tzu* was the Ruling Star of the year, his vapor was conceived. In the first year, named *chia-shen*, of the reign of the Emperor of Peace, his shape took form. During the seventh year of the High Harmony, named *keng-yin*, on the third day, named *chia-tzu*, at the hour of *mao*, when virtue and body were in union and the stars were aligned, he was conceived in the Jade Kingdom of the Mysterious North, in the spirit realm of the celestial bodies, on the mountain of Peng-lai that was shaped part human and part bird, in the valley of the *li* trees.

There was a virgin who was the mother of the High Mysteries who lived in the Chamber of the Nine Mysteries, deep within the shady (yin) valley. When the Mysterious Virgin conceived, she saw in a dream the infant's body wrapped in the clouds, the sun, and the moon. The six breaths resonated with his spirit. She felt the movement of yang and knew that she carried within her womb an enlightened being.

On the morning of his birthday, three suns rose from the east. After he suckled, magic water came out of the mouths of nine dragons. That is why the people of that spirit valley gave it the name "bright landscape."

By the beginning of his third year, his body had attained the true form, and his speech radiated a golden splendor. At five, he frequently gazed at the sun and smiled, and looked at the moon and sighed. Up above he observed the growth of the breath of yang. Down below he saw the way of yin and waning. Therefore he cared for his spirit and harmonized his soul. He held on to the fetus to keep his spirit sacred. He gathered generative energy to fill his blood. He strengthened his marrow to build his tendons.

At seven he learned to swallow the rays of light, eat the mist, and chew the tendrils of the sun. At the age of twenty-seven, his complexion radiated a golden glow. Leaving the mundane world and distancing himself from desire, he pledged to save the world. His spirit moved the Lords of the Great Primal Beginning and he was given the teachings of the Three Completenesses. He practiced the teachings of the Three Caverns and his deeds were seen in the nine directions. At thirty-seven, he could use his humility and simplicity to file down sharpness. At forty-seven, he could use his throat to gather the harmonious light. At fifty-seven, his saliva became the mysterious nectar and his works of merit traveled everywhere unhindered. At sixty-seven, he gave a treatise to the Latter Sacred Lord, who was also the Lord who had received the Tao before sky and earth were created. He is named the Latter Sacred Lord because that was how it was recorded. The Earlier Sacred and Latter Sacred are really the same [sic].

He then ascended to the Palace of the High Pure and wandered in the Houses of T'ai-chi. He rules the skies and the ten realms below. He is given jurisdiction over the millions of mortal beings. He watches over the sky, rivers, seas, plains, valleys, mountains, and woods. There is none that will not obey him. He is the judge of the nine levels and ten layers. Therefore he is called the Nine Mysteries.

At seventy, his longevity became limitless. He could
hide and appear with ease. He has mastered the arts of
immortality and compiled the methods and formulae of
longevity.

## NOTES ON THE TRANSLATION

Taoist religious terms can be intimidating to people who are
not familiar with them, so some of the terminology from
the selection is explained below.

The One True Wonderful Vapor is also known as the
Breath of the Tao, the Primordial Vapor, and the Undifferentiated Vapor. These are all names of the Tao, the origin
and underlying reality of all things. In the *T'ai-p'ing ching*
the term also refers to the ideal state of existence, when
everything was in the embrace of the Tao.

Taoist celestial space is divided into nine layers, called
the Nine Mysteries. The Ninth Mystery is the highest layer
of the celestial realm. In the *T'ai-p'ing ching*, the High Pure
Golden Tower of Sky is the entrance to Shang-ch'ing, the
domain of the highest deities. The Golden Tower is sometimes called the Mysterious Gate. Later, the High Pure
(Shang-ch'ing) Realm was replaced by the Jade Pure (Yü-
ch'ing) Realm as the highest level of the celestial domain.

The passage of time in the Chinese calendar is reckoned
by a system called the Ten Celestial Stems and Twelve Terrestrial Branches. The Ten Celestial Stems are *chia, i, ping,
ting, wu, chi, keng, hsin, jen*, and *kuei*. The Twelve Terrestrial Branches are *tzu, ch'ou, yin, mao, ch'en, ssu, wu, wei*,

*shen*, *yu*, *hsü*, and *hai*. Each year, month, and day can be designated by a pair of stem and branch. Thus, in the text, *ping-tzu* and *keng-yin* identify the year, and *chia-tzu* identifies the day. The Ruling Star of a year is also named after the stem-branch combination. The Ruling Star of the year is a controller of events of that year. It is also the Guardian Star of all persons born in that year. The day is divided into twelve two-hour units, and each unit is named after a Terrestrial Branch.

The Jade Kingdom of the Mysterious North is the realm of the North Pole Star and the Constellation of the Northern Bushel (the Big Dipper). The highest deities are said to reside in these stars.

The fetus of the Great Void refers to the spirit or seed of immortality. It also means the "son of the Mother (the Tao)." In the text, it is taken to mean that Lao-tzu's mother is the Tao itself.

Finally, the nine levels and ten layers refer to the nine steps of the celestial realm and the ten levels of the underworld. The Taoist underworld, at least in the period when the *T'ai-p'ing ching* was written, was not a hell. It resembles a shaman's otherworld where the Taoist journeyed in spirit to rescue a sick person's soul or obtain power from the Guardians of the Tao.

### Pei-tou yen-sheng ching
#### (*The North Star Scripture of Longevity*)

The full title of this scripture is *T'ai-shang hsüan-ling pei-tou pen-ming yen-sheng chen-ching*. Translated, it means "the True Scripture of the North Star, the Governor of Longevity and Destiny, as revealed by the Sacred Spirit of the Great One." Although the text says that the scripture was revealed by Lao-tzu to the Celestial Teacher Chang Taoling, it is now generally agreed that the book was written sometime during the end of the T'ang and the beginning of the Sung dynasty.

The *Pei-tou yen-sheng ching* is a liturgy. It is meant to be chanted in a service accompanied by rituals or read aloud at home by devotees. The *Pei-tou yen-sheng ching* is also one of the most popular liturgies of Taoism. This liturgy is typically chanted on the first and fifteenth day of the lunar month and on the Festival of the Northern Bushel Stars, which falls on the first nine days of the ninth lunar month. Because the North Star and the Northern Bushel Stars are associated with longevity, the *Pei-tou yen-sheng ching* is also chanted as a birthday blessing.

## *From the* Pei-tou yen-sheng ching

### Prologue

On the seventh day of the first month in the first year of the Realm of Everlasting Life, the Patriarch Lao-tzu was in the Palace of T'ai-chi in the Realm of T'ai-ch'ing (Great Purity). He looked at sentient beings and saw that for millennia they had been sunk into the depths of suffering, doomed to repeat countless cycles of rebirth. Whether born human, whether born on Chinese soil, in foreign lands, or in underdeveloped countries, whether born rich or poor, everyone lived on borrowed time. Many souls had fallen into the underworld, wandering without peace, their destruction brought about by their evil deeds. They were imprisoned in the world of the dead and suffered greater torment than they could bear. They would never find human existence again and would be reborn as beasts, birds, and insects. Having left the path of humanity, it would be difficult for them to return to it. However, despite all this, they still did not awaken. They were locked into the cycles of rebirth because they had been ignorant in their previous lifetimes.

Lao-tzu, out of great compassion, took on human form and descended to the mortal realm to teach humanity. In the capital city of the Kingdom of Shu, the guardian of the earth rose from the ground and built a jade platform. The Patriarch Lao-tzu ascended the platform and transmitted the Scripture of the North Star to the Celestial Master, telling him to let this scripture be known far and wide, so that people might be delivered from their sufferings.

## THE MAIN SECTION

The Patriarch Lao-tzu said to the Celestial Master:

"It is difficult to be born in human form. It is even more difficult to be born in the central lands. Even if you have that opportunity, to encounter the true teaching is rare. Many are lost in delusion. Many stray into evil paths. Many are deeply rooted in their unethical ways. Many are dishonest and dishonorable. Many kill and rape. Many delight in casual pleasures. Many are greedy and jealous. Many souls are lost in the underworld. Many have lost their chance to exist in human form. Humanity does not understand karma. They do not know the true way. They are confused and lost. Seeing the suffering of humanity, I am moved by compassion to give them these teachings. I will let them know that all life comes from the Tao. If they understand this, then they will attain longevity. Their seed will not die. They will continue to exist in human form. They will not be born in lands where the teachings of the Tao are unknown. They will not lose the essence of being human. Moreover, they will cultivate the Tao in themselves and gradually enter the path of immortality. They will be liberated from the cycles of rebirth. They will transcend earthly existence and merge with the Tao. This is why I want to give you this great and wonderful vehicle, so that you can deliver humanity, and let them return to their true nature.

"On their birthday, they should abstain from meat, conduct a ceremony, and make offerings to the Northern Bushel deities, the Three Lords and Five Emperors, the Nine Officers and the Four Magistrates. At this time they can ask for blessings and deliverance from catastrophes. They can present petitions and sincerely ask for forgiveness. They should offer fragrant flowers and five kinds of fresh fruits. Following the ways of the sky and earth, they should make the offerings seriously and formally, purifying the environment where the ceremony is held. Whether the ceremony is conducted in a temple or at home, the effects of their actions will be felt. If they perform the ceremony they will receive merit. Remember, do not forget this and do not be tardy.

"Chanting the names of the Northern Bushel deities can deliver you from disaster. It can ward off evil and give you prosperity and longevity. It can help you accumulate good deeds. If you feel that a disaster is imminent, light incense and chant the North Star Mantra, and it will give you peace of mind. I shall now transmit this chant to you:

> The seven sacred deities of the Northern Bushel
> Can deliver us from the three disasters;
> The seven sacred deities of the Northern Bushel
> Can deliver us from the four destructive forces;
> The seven sacred deities of the Northern Bushel
> Can deliver us from catastrophes of the five elements;
> The seven sacred deities of the Northern Bushel
> Can deliver us from the six harms;
> The seven sacred deities of the Northern Bushel
> Can deliver us from the seven injuries;
> The seven sacred deities of the Northern Bushel
> Can deliver us from the eight obstacles;
> The seven sacred deities of the Northern Bushel
> Can deliver us from the nine baleful stars;
> The seven sacred deities of the Northern Bushel
> Can dissolve the disharmony between husband and
>     wife;
> The seven sacred deities of the Northern Bushel

Can dissolve the conflicts between men and women;
The seven sacred deities of the Northern Bushel
Can protect you from problems in pregnancy and birth;
The seven sacred deities of the Northern Bushel
Can deliver you from the cycles of rebirth;
The seven sacred deities of the Northern Bushel
Can ward off the disaster of epidemics;
The seven sacred deities of the Northern Bushel
Can ward off the disaster of illness;
The seven sacred deities of the Northern Bushel
Can ward off evil spirits;
The seven sacred deities of the Northern Bushel
Can ward off the attacks of tigers and wolves;
The seven sacred deities of the Northern Bushel
Can ward off the attacks of poisonous insects and
    snakes;
The seven sacred deities of the Northern Bushel
Can ward off the attacks of thieves and robbers;
The seven sacred deities of the Northern Bushel
Can protect you from accidental punishment;
The seven sacred deities of the Northern Bushel
Can protect you from accidental death;
The seven sacred deities of the Northern Bushel
Can protect you from misfortune coming from curses;
The seven sacred deities of the Northern Bushel
Can protect you from disasters coming from the skies;
The seven sacred deities of the Northern Bushel
Can protect you from disasters on the ground;
The seven sacred deities of the Northern Bushel

Can protect you from disasters coming from wars;
The seven sacred deities of the Northern Bushel
Can protect you from disasters of fire and water.
The lords of the seven stars
Are compassionate and understanding.
They deliver us from all disasters
And liberate us from suffering.
If you are beset with problems,
Chant these lines and it will give you peace.
You will be filled with great fortune
And will be in harmony with the five elements.
Your three souls will be healthy and stable,
And evil will stay away forever.
The true breath will descend from the five directions,
And many great fortunes will come to you.

"The names of the true lords of the stars are seldom uttered or heard. If you chant them, the Tao will grow strong and deep in you. It is good karma that led you to know them. If you chant their names, you will accumulate merits beyond measure. When honest men and women chant this scripture, their wisdom and original nature will develop. The heart of Tao will be opened. They will leave the path of delusion and enter the Gate of the Rare Mystery. They will return to the true way and enter the immortal realm.

"Therefore, during the festivals of the Lords of the Three Realms and the eight celebrations, your birthday, and the days in which the deities of the Seven Stars descend to earth, you should prepare an altar, chant this scripture, perform the ceremony, and abstain from meat. Follow the procedures carefully and your prosperity will know no measure. In every lifetime the sacred truth will not abandon you. You will not enter paths of evil. Those who possess this scripture can also regularly chant the names of the Lords of the Seven Stars. In this way, they will accumulate merit and fortune will descend on them.

"This is the sacred mantra:

The North Star group has nine luminous bodies.
In the center of the sky is the great sacred star:
Upward it points toward the golden gate,
Downward it envelops the Kun-lun mountains.
It regulates the movement of all things
And rules the universe.
The Great Pivot,
The Star Craving Wolf,
The Great Gate Star,
The Star of Prosperity,
The Scholar Star,
The Star of Virtue,
The Warrior Star,
The Destroyer of Enemies,
The Jade Emperor's star on high,
Which is the purple throne of the great lord.
The celestial circle of the macrocosm
Is present in the microcosm of a grain of dust.
Is there any disaster that it cannot avert?

Is there any prosperity that it cannot grant?
Let the true vapor of the ancient emperor
Come to protect my body.
All the constellations rotate around the Celestial Pivot,
Day and night without stopping.
We, the unworthy, who live in the mortal realm,
Are drawn toward the Tao and ask for enlightenment.
We are willing to abide by the solemnity of the ritual
So that we may attain immortality.
The Three Altar Stars: Energy of the Void,
The Scholar and Warrior Stars that give me balance—
From them I am born;
From them I receive nourishment;
They protect my human form."

## NOTES ON THE TRANSLATION

The three disasters are catastrophes that come from the sky, the earth, and water. The four destructive forces are the *sha* (mischievous and harmful spirits) coming from the four directions: north, south, east, and west. The catastrophes of the five elements are accidents involving metal, wood, water, fire, and earth.

The six harms come from the six senses: eyes, ears, nose, tongue, body, and mind. Because of desire, the six senses are attached to objects. Attachment to objects of desire drains internal energy, leading to the loss of health and longevity.

The seven injuries come from excessive responses of the

seven emotions: happiness, anger, sorrow, fear, elatedness, likes, and dislikes. The seven emotions are linked to the seven souls, or *p'o*. Indulgence in these emotions will lead to the loss of the seven *p'o*. This affects mental stability since insanity is often described as the dissolution of the seven *p'o*. It also affects physical health because emotional outbursts and fluctuation of moods are harmful to the internal organs and the circulation of internal energy.

When the three disasters are mentioned with the nine catastrophes, they refer to the three blockages in the cavities along the spinal column. The three disasters are sometimes called "the three poisons" because the three blockages can hinder the circulation of energy and cause illness. The nine catastrophes are the nine closures in the cavities along the spinal column. The closures can drain energy away from an individual, block the flow of energy in the body, and cause illness.

# 4

## *The Tao Within*

### Mystical Taoism

THE GOAL OF THE MYSTIC IS TO BE united with the greater or cosmic part of the self. Shang-ch'ing Taoism, which emerged in China in the third and fourth centuries CE, is a form of mystical Taoism where the cosmic part of the self is the Tao. The primordial energy of the Tao is present in both the macrocosm of nature and the microcosm of the human body. By visualizing the images of the deities and journeying to their realms in the sun, moon, and stars, the Shang-ch'ing mystics achieved an ecstatic union with the greater power that is resident in the universe and within themselves. These two aspects of the Taoist mystical experience are illustrated by the two most important texts of Shang-ch'ing Taoism: *The Shang-ch'ing Huang-t'ing nei-ching yü-ching* (The Yellow Court Jade Classic of the Internal Images of the High Pure Realm), and the *Shang-ch'ing chin-ch'üeh ti-chün wu-tou san-yüan t'u-chüeh* (The Lord of the Golden Tower of the High Pure Realm's Illustrated Instructions on [Visualizing] the Five Bushels and the Three Ones).

## Shang-ch'ing huang-t'ing nei-ching yü-ching
### (*The Yellow Court Jade Classic of the Internal Images of the High Pure Realm*)

The *Shang-ch'ing huang-t'ing nei-ching yü-ching* is regarded as *the* representative scripture of Shang-ch'ing Taoism. Reputed to have been revealed by the deities to Lady Wei Hua-ts'un in 288 CE, the scripture was passed on to Yang Hsi, who transmitted it to Hsü Hui and Hsü Mi. When Lu Hsiu-ching compiled the Taoist books into the Three Caverns in 471 CE, the *Huang-t'ing nei-ching yü-ching* became a part of the Taoist canon.

This scripture is a revealed text. Revealed texts are meant to carry an authority greater than texts written by mortals. One can tell whether a scripture is a revealed text by looking at its preface or the first few lines. Revealed texts always name the deity who transmitted the text to the writer. This is typically followed by statements of why the text is important.

There are two *Huang-t'ing ching*s: the *Huang-t'ing nei-ching yü-ching* (The Yellow Court Jade Classic of Internal Images) and the *Huang-t'ing wai-ching yü-ching* (The Yellow Court Jade Classic of External Images). The former is an esoteric text and the latter is an exoteric text. In spiritual literature, esoteric texts are written for initiates and exoteric texts are written for the general public. That the contents of the *Wai-ching* are almost entirely contained in the *Nei-ching* suggests that the former is probably an introductory text while the latter contains secret teachings available only to the initiated.

Personally, I find the *Nei-ching* very much like an instruction manual and the *Wai-ching* more like a description of the internal universe of the human body. My own training in internal alchemy has helped me to decode much of the information contained in the *Nei-ching*. The phrases of the *Nei-ching* text are stylistically similar to instruction mnemonics (*k'ou-chüeh*) that my Taoist teachers have given me.

## *The Origin and Transmission of the* Huang-t'ing nei-ching yü-ching

### PREFACE

The Great Lord of Fu-sang ordered the immortal King of the Yang Valley to transmit to Lady Wei the *Huang-t'ing nei-ching yü-ching*. It is called the Great High's Harmonious Writ of the Heart. It is called the Golden Book of the Great Lord. It is called the Jade Scroll of the Lord of the East.

After purifying yourself for ninety days, recite it ten thousand times. It will harmonize the three human spirits (*hun*), refine the seven souls (*p'o*), eradicate the three monsters, and sooth and harmonize the five viscera. Your complexion will glow with color; you will be like an infant; the hundred illnesses cannot harm you, and disasters cannot overwhelm you.

After you have recited it ten thousand times, you will naturally see the spirits and deities in the cavern, and will be able to look internally at the intestines and stomach and see the five viscera. At that time, an enlightened being of the Yellow Court, the Jade Lady of the Center, will teach you how to live forever. These are the teachings of immortality.

You who have the mark of an immortal, receive my text. This text displays the one true form of the immortal spirit's abode where the sacred fetus dwells. To those who recite this text, the immortal spirit's dwelling place will be bright and strong, the true fetus will be safe and still, the sacred nectar will flow smoothly, the hundred gates will be bright and clear, the blood and marrow will be plentiful, the intestines and stomach will be empty yet full, there will be luster in the five viscera, the ears and eyes will be intelligent, broken teeth will become new, and the white hair will become black. Because I can eradicate evil and confusion, this is why I have been given the true names of the spirits of the six orbs.

When form is full and the spirit is strong, you will not die even if you want to. This is why the Inner Chapters of the *Huang-ting ching* contains the teachings of immortality.

## Chapter 1: The High Pure (Shang-ch'ing) Realm

Before the Purple Cloud of the Emperor of the Void in the High Pure Realm, the Lord of the Jade Dawn of the Great Way secluded himself in the Chamber of the Pearl Medicine and wrote these seven-word phrases:

Spreading the five forms and transforming them into the
   ten thousand spirits:
This is described in the Inner Chapters of the *Huang-
   ting ching*.
The harmonious music in the center is played in the
   three registers to accompany the dance of the
   immortal fetus.
Nine vapors shine brightly from the highest places.
From the child's spirit brow a purple haze is born.
This Jade Text is extraordinary and exquisite.
Recite it ten thousand times and you will rise to the
   three celestial realms.
A thousand disasters will go away and a hundred
   illnesses will be cured.
You will not be afraid of fierce tigers and brutal wolves;
Old age will be taken away and you will live forever.


# *The Guardian Spirits of the Body*


## CHAPTER 7: ATTAINING THE TAO

Attaining the Tao is not difficult if you are sincere.
The Mud Ball cavity and the hundred joints all have spirits.
Black and white, the spirit of hairs is called Great
   Beginning;
Root of vitality, the spirit of the brain is called Mud Ball;
High up and bright, the spirit of the eyes is called
   Mysterious Infant;

Protruding like a piece of jade, the spirit of the nose is
    called Hard Numinous Spirit;
Empty yet closed, the spirit of the eye is called Quiet Field;
Connected to life itself, the spirit of the tongue is called
    Judge of Principles;
Tough and sharp, the spirit of teeth is called a Thousand
    Varieties.
The spirit of the face is governed by the Mud Ball.
The Nine Cavities of the Mud Ball all have chambers.
The circle with the one-inch square is located here.
Swallow the Purple Robe and fly to the Palace of
    Multiplicities.
Contemplate this once and your longevity will have no end.
Everything is inside the brain.
All the spirits are seated, facing outward.
Keep them in your mind and they will naturally respond.

## CHAPTER 8: SPIRIT OF THE HEART

The spirit of the heart, the Beginning of the elixir, is called
    Holding the Numinous Spirit;
The spirit of the lungs, a grand cover, is called Complete
    Emptiness;
The spirit of the liver, with the dragon's vapor, is called
    Containing Brightness;
Like burning wood, it directs the smoke to separate the
    muddy from the clear.
The spirit of the kidneys, mysterious and dark, is called
    Nourishing the Infant;

The spirit of the spleen, which is always present, is called
    Restrainer of the human spirits;
The spirit of the gallbladder, like a shining dragon, is called
    Strong Brilliance.
The spirits of six bowels and five viscera are integral to
    vitality.
Follow their path of celestial movements in your mind.
Keep them inside day and night and you will naturally live
    a long life.

### NOTES ON THE TRANSLATION

There is a lot of symbolism in the text. To explain and inter-
pret each term would be beyond the scope of this book.
However, some Chinese words have no simple English
equivalents and need some clarification on how they are
translated. I have translated the Chinese word *shen* as
spirit, *ling* as numinous spirit, and *hun* as human spirit.
Some writers have rendered all three Chinese words as
spirit. If these words do not appear together in the same
segment of text, it is viable to translate any one of them as
spirit. However, in the *Huang-t'ing ching*, all three words—
*shen*, *ling*, and *hun*—often appear together, and it would
be confusing if all of them were translated the same.

    I chose to translate *shen* as spirit because traditionally
the Chinese meaning for shen is a spirit that is an entity. I
feel that the *shen* in the Taoist scriptures have this nature.
They are immortal, though they are guardian spirits inside
us. I have translated *ling* as "numinous spirit" because *ling*

has the connotation of "brightness and intelligence". For *hun*, I have used the term "human spirit" to distinguish it from the immortal spirit, for the *hun* is intimately tied to a mortal being. It resides in the human body when the individual is alive; it leaves the body at death, and depending on one's religious belief, it may wander in the underworld or enter another body to be reborn. In Taoism, the *shen* are spirits that protect and judge us, the *ling* are spirits that teach us, and the *hun* are spirits that are wayward and mischievous. I hope that translating the three words in this manner will clarify their Taoist meanings.

*The* Shang-ch'ing chin-ch'üeh ti-chün wu-tou
san-yüan t'u-chüeh
*(The Lord of the Golden Tower of the High Pure
Realm's Illustrated Instructions on [Visualizing]
the Five Bushels and the Three Ones)*

This is one of the many Shang-ch'ing scriptures collected in the Taoist canon said to be transmitted by the deity Lord Chou, whose full title is Tzu-yang Chen-jen Chou-chün (The Immortal Lord Chou of the Purple Light).

The text contains instructions for visualizing the deities and merging with them in their celestial palaces. The excerpt below describes the procedure for visualizations performed at the spring equinox. The complete text in the Taoist canon contains procedures for the summer solstice, autumn equinox, and winter solstice, as well as various days of the month.

## *Flying to the Stars*

At the beginning of midnight at spring equinox, sit with your eyes closed and face east. Keep me within your body along with the Three Palaces, the Three Ones, and the Three Officials. Together with the Seven, and me in the center, ride the smoke of the purple vapor and step up to the Northern Bushel's (Big Dipper's) Bright Star. The Bright Daylight Star is the Eastern Deity of the Bushel. In this way, you will be transported to the center of the stars. Sit and inhale the purple vapor thirty times. Soon you will see the Eastern High Palace of the Bright Daylight Star. Inside the Palace is the Child of the Green Mystery who will give you the True Light. First, keep the big web of purple vapor below the North Star in front of me. Then hold on to the Three Ones.

These are the oral instructions from the deities.

The Deity Lord Chou said: Hold on to the seven figures and the mantle of the Bushel or the Seven Stars and rise with them to the Brilliant Daylight. Traveling with my lord in the center on the star mantle, turn the head of the handle so that the First Star is pointing forward. Inhale the purple vapor thirty times, keeping me in the purple haze while you are inhaling. Now visualize the Three Ones and the Three Officials. When you have finished inhaling, you should see seven figures revolving around in the purple haze as they descend into the Three Palaces. After a period of time, recite this petition in your mind:

The Thrice Honored Truly Highest Lord Above of the
    Great Mystery, Brilliant Daylight;
Ruler of spring when the thousand children open the
    gates to complete the elixir;
Ruler of the summer's pearly vapor mixed with the
    smoke of the feminine generative energy;
Ruler of the autumn's celestial splendor, the six
    constellations and the North Pole;
Ruler of the winter when the ten thousand evils block
    and rape the five earths—*keng, jen, wu, chi.*
Let the Celestial Barriers crumble and dissolve when I
    turn to face them;
Refine my seven souls and my three human spirits;
Give life to my five viscera;
Let me attain the real, fly to the High Pure Realm's
    floating images of the Seven Beginnings, live long,
    and follow my nature.
After my long cry to the thousand spirits,
Let me rest and keep within me the four seasons.
This is my sole wish.

**NOTES ON THE TRANSLATION**

Again there is quite a bit of esoteric symbolism here, and
to explain each symbol would be beyond the scope of this
book. To be consistent with the *Huang-t'ing nei-ching yü-
ching*, I have translated *hun* as human spirit although it is
the only "spirit" mentioned in this text. I have also translated the words *yin ching* as "feminine generative energy"

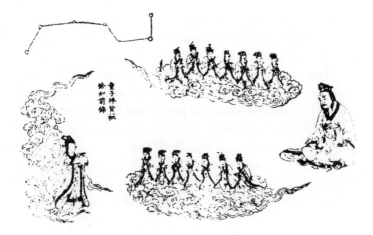

*From the text* Shang-ch'ing chin-ch'üeh ti-chün wu-tou san-yüan t'u-chüeh *(The Lord of the Golden Tower of the High Pure Realm's Illustrated Instructions on [Visualizing] the Five Bushels and the Three Ones). The Shang-ch'ing adept sits at the right, and the seven celestial lords of the Northern Bushel are in the center. The figure on the left is the young attendant who brings messages from the celestial lords to the practitioner.*

because in the text it is paired with the "pearly vapor," which is male generative energy.

The pronoun "me" in the expression "keeping me within" refers to the guardian deity, the numinous spirit, and the energy of life inside us. The text consists of words spoken by the deity to the practitioner. Thus, "you," the practitioner, need to keep "me," the deity, within. If "you" lose "me," you will lose the connection to life.

*Keng, jen, wu, chi,* are four Celestial Stems. For a discussion of the Celestial Stems, please refer to the Translation Notes in chapter 3 (page 55). The text here mentions five and lists four because the first stem, *chia,* is "hidden" (*tun*). This is common knowledge to Taoist practitioners, although it is somewhat confusing to people unfamiliar with divinational arcana in Taoism. The scope of this book does not allow me to explain the meaning "hiding the *chia* stem" in detail. Briefly, there are two accepted meanings. One is that *chia,* as a Celestial Stem and stellar body, is hidden because it can take on many possible positions. Its location cannot be determined when the rest of the Stems are fitted into the *pa-k'ua* (eight trigrams). The second meaning is that *chia* refers to a dark or invisible star, which embodies the primal darkness or the essence of yin energy. Like the dark side of the moon, it is hidden and cannot be seen.

# 5

## *In Search of Immortality*

### TAOIST INTERNAL ALCHEMY

S KY AND EARTH ARE AGELESS BECAUSE they are constantly renewed by the breath of the Tao, the source of life. If humans can cultivate the breath of the Tao and circulate it in the body, they too can become immortal and be at one with the sky and earth. Cultivating and circulating the energy of the Tao require transforming body and mind so that the energy within is as pristine as that of the primordial vapor of the Tao. This process of transformation is likened to refining metals, and the methods of purifying body and mind are known as "alchemy."

The selections in this chapter are from two classics of Taoist alchemy: the *Tsan-tung-chi* (Triplex Unity), and the *Wu-jen p'ien* (Understanding Reality).

### Tsan-tung-chi (Triplex Unity)

The *Tsan-tung-chi* is regarded by Taoists as the ancestor of all alchemical literature and is reputed to have been written by Wei Po-yang, the father of Taoist alchemy. The oldest sections of the book have been dated to 142 CE. The phrase *tsan-tung-chi* can be interpreted in several ways. Briefly, *tsan* means combining, *tung* means similar, and *chi* means bringing together. Literally, the phrase means "to compound together three similar substances." Some commentators of the *Tsan-tung-chi* have interpreted the three substances to be the three internal energies: *ching* (generative energy), *ch'i* (vital or breath), and *shen* (spirit). Others have chosen to describe them as lead, mercury, and cinnabar. Yet others have described them as the Three Ones, who are the guardians of the three energy fields (called *tan-t'ien*s) in the body. The Three have also been referred to as the three realms of existence: sky, earth, and humanity (or heaven, earth, and man). The diverse interpretations of the title of the book suggest that the *Tsan-tung-chi* has many levels of meaning. It is simultaneously a theory of the human body, a set of guidelines for spiritual transformation, and a manual for cultivating health.

Historians and scholars now agree that the *Tsan-tung-chi* in the Taoist canon is probably the work of several authors. Some parts of the *Tsan-tung-chi* are written in the poetic style of four beats to the line and some with five beats. Other parts are written in prose. It is now generally accepted that the middle section of the book was written by Wei Po-yang himself in the second century CE. Some parts were added by his students, and some sections were probably written by practitioners of Taoist alchemy as late as the sixth century CE.

My translation of the *Tsan-tung-chi* is from the version collected in the Cheng-t'ung Taoist canon (ca. 1440s). I have kept the partitions used by the major commentators. Richard Bertschinger's *The Secret of Everlasting Life* presents the *Tsan-tung-chi* in a different order. Bertschinger's translation is from the *Ku-wen tsan-tung-chi* (The Old Text of the Triplex Unity). Although the *Ku-wen* text was once regarded as a secret version that is older than the *Tsan-tung-chi* of the Taoist canon, scholars have now determined that the *Ku-wen* text was actually written during the reign of Emperor Chang Te (1506–1521 CE) of the Ming dynasty. This means the *Kun-wen* text actually postdates the one collected in the Taoist Canon.

Regardless of when it was written and who contributed to its authorship, the *Tsan-tung-chi* is a remarkable work. Today, fifteen hundred years after Wei Po-yang first set down his theory and practice of transforming body and mind, the *Tsan-tung-chi* is still acknowledged by Taoists as the definitive manual of spiritual transformation.

## Cultivating Mind

From Part One

Nourish yourself internally.
In peace, stillness, and complete emptiness,
The hidden light of the origin will glow
To illuminate the entire body.

Close and block the mouth
To strengthen the numinous pearl.
Let the three lights sink below
To incubate the young pearl.
Look for it and you cannot see it.
Yet it is close by and easy to get.
As the Yellow Center gradually penetrates everything,
Luster and glow will spread to the muscles and skin.
Start your cultivation correctly and you will be able to see
    it to completion.
The trunk will stand firm and the branches will take hold.
The One is concealed and hidden;
The people of the world have never known it.
Great virtue does not act;
It does not seek or want.
Lesser virtue acts;
And it is used endlessly.
Great obstruction is called "having";
No obstruction is called "nothingness."
Nothingness can carry you up
To where the sacred virtue resides.
This is the method of the "dual-entrance cavity"
In which gold and energy (ch'i) work together.

## Cultivating Body

### From Part Two

The mirror of yang makes fire,
But if there is no sun, it will not give light.
If not for the moon and the stars,
How can the watery fluid be collected?
If two energies that are distant from each other
Can respond and communicate,
How much more can those that are close, inside your body,
And held within your chest?
Match yin and yang to the sun and moon,
And use fire and water to activate each other.
The three treasures—ears, eyes, and mouth—
Close and block them and let nothing through.
The enlightened being is immersed in the depths,
Floating and wandering, keeping the direction within.
Sight and hearing are devious and crooked.
Opening and closing must be synchronized.
In the pivot and axle of the self,
Movement and stillness must never be exhausted.
Guard the energy of *li* (fire) within.
Do not tax the intelligent energy of *k'an* (water).
Close the mouth and stop talking;
To speak rarely is to flow with the undifferentiated whole.
These are the three important principles:
Relax your body and situate yourself in an empty room;

Abandon the will, and return to the void and nothingness.
When there are no thoughts, you will find the constant.
Let difficulties prod you forward.
Focus the mind and do not let it wander.
Embrace the spirit when you sleep.
Attend to its care and beware of its neglect.
Your complexion will be moistened until it is shining;
The bones and joints will grow firm and strong.
When all the toxins are discharged,
The true yang will stand up alone.
Cultivate without stopping,
And the mass of energy will move like cloud and rain.
Flowing like spring showers,
Dripping like melting ice,
From the head falling down to the feet,
And from there rising up again,
Coming and going, swirling the limitless,
And stirring everything throughout.
Those on the path of the return know the Tao.
Weakness is the handle of virtue.
Plow and pull out the weeds of impurity.
Do it meticulously and you will attain harmony.
For in the mud lies a clear path,
And in the long darkness a light will finally shine through.
People of the world love little tricks.
They do not probe the depths of the Tao.
They abandon the correct way and follow the devious
    paths.
They want the quick way but they do not get through.

Like the blind leaning on a staff,
Like the deaf who hear ringing in the ears,
They go under the water to hunt for birds and rabbits;
They climb the mountains to look for fish and dragon;
They plant wheat and hope to harvest millet;
They swing a compass to draw a square;
They exhaust their strength and weary the spirit,
And at the end of their lives there is no attainment.
If you want to know how to feed on internal energy,
The procedure is not really that complicated.


## *The Alchemical Process*

From Part Two

Strive to nourish your inner nature;
Lengthen your life and turn back time.
Consider the final outcome;
And think about what came before.
We are endowed with a body
Whose form is fundamentally empty.
The primordial generative energy spreads like a cloud,
Held up by vapor in the Beginning.
Yin and yang are the bases of things,
Coming to reside within as *hun* (human spirit) and *p'o*
    (soul).
The yang spirit of the sun is the human spirit,
The yin spirit of the moon is the soul.

Joining together, the human spirit and the soul
Live with each other in the same home.
The inner nature rules within,
Setting up its position in the castle.
Feelings rule the camp outside,
Building and strengthening the city wall.
When the city and its walls are complete,
The people will be secure.
At the appointed time,
Feelings are united with *ch'ien* (sky) and *k'un* (earth).
When *ch'ien* moves, it becomes erect;
The vapor spreads as the generative energy flows.
When *k'un* is still, it contracts;
Becoming the furnace in the lodge of the Tao.
Apply firmness, then withdraw;
Transform it into softness to provide stimulation.
The Nine is circulated, the Seven is cycled in reverse;
The Eight returns, and the Six stays within.
Male is white, female is red.
Gold and water embrace each other.
Water stabilizes fire,
And the cycle of the five elements is started.
The highest good is like water;
It is clear without a blemish.
The true form of the Tao
And its Oneness is hard to describe.
It changes and spreads,
The parts settling by themselves.
It resembles a chicken's egg,

Where black and white are bound together.
It is about one inch wide
When it first begins.
Then the four limbs and five viscera,
The tendons and bones become complete.
After ten months,
It slips out of the womb.
The bones are soft and curled,
And its flesh is slippery like polished lead.


## Immortality

From Part Three

The sages and wise ones
Carried the mystery and embraced the ultimate reality.
They refined the Nine Cauldrons,
Covered their traces, and hid from the world.
They conserved their generative energy, nourished the
    spirit,
And understood the value of the Three Primal Ones.
The sweet nectar moistened their skin and flesh,
Their tendons and bones were soft and strong.
They expelled all the toxins from the body,
And constantly preserved their true energy.
Having accumulated these effects over a long time,
Their bodies were transformed, and they became
    immortals.

**NOTES ON THE TRANSLATION**

There are many symbols in the *Tsan-tung-chi*. This kind of symbolic reference is quite common in the texts of internal alchemy. To explain the meaning of each line in the text is beyond the scope of this book. Readers who want to know more about the language of Taoist alchemy can refer to my books *The Shambhala Guide to Taoism* and *Harmonizing Yin and Yang: The Dragon-Tiger Classic* (forthcoming).

I have retained the Chinese words of *ch'ien*, *k'un*, *k'an*, and *li* in the translation instead of substituting them with the English *sky*, *earth*, *water*, and *fire* because these Chinese terms have unique meanings. Thus, for example, *k'an* is not simply water, but water of the *pa-k'ua*, which is different from water of the five elements.

Although the *Tsan-tung-chi* was written as a manual, it is not to be taken casually as a "how to" book. Even if you are familiar with Taoist alchemy, you should not use it as a manual without supervision and guidance from a teacher.

## *The* Wu-jen p'ien *(Understanding Reality)*

The *Wu-jen p'ien* was written by Chang Po-tuan, who was one of the greatest theorists and adepts of Taoist alchemy in the Northern Sung dynasty (960–1126 CE).

The alchemical procedures described in the *Wu-jen p'ien* are similar to those outlined in the *Tsan-tung-chi*, except for one major difference. For Wei Po-yang and the alchemists of his time, the ingestion of minerals (external alchemy) was perfectly compatible with using internal methods to transform body and mind (internal alchemy). On the other hand, Chang Po-tuan believed that all the ingredients of alchemical transformation are found in the body and that there is no need to ingest minerals and herbs.

## *The Process of Internal Alchemy*

From Part One

### 3

If you want to attain immortality, make sure it is celestial
    immortality.
Only the Golden Elixir (Pill) is the best.
When the two come together, feelings and inner nature
    merge.
Where the five elements gather, the dragon and tiger
    copulate.
With earth yang (*wu*) and earth yin (*chi*) as go-betweens,
Husband and wife happily join together.
Wait for the work to complete and then present yourself
    before the jade tower,
Borne on the flying phoenix in the light of the nine mists.

### 4

This wonderful method is the most real of the real.
It solely depends on oneself and not on others.
Know the inversion of *li* (fire) and *k'an* (water) within.

Who knows if it is floating or sinking, or who is host or
     guest?
If you want to hold the mercury within the cinnabar and
     keep both of them inside the golden cauldron,
First put into the jade pond the silver within the water.
In the spiritual work, it does not take a whole day to pump
     the fires,
Before the disk of the sun appears in the jade pool.


6

Everyone originally has the medicine of longevity within.
However, they have lost their understanding and thrown it
     away.
When the sweet dew descends, sky and earth will be
     joined.
The place where the yellow sprouts grow is where *k'an* and
     *li* interact.
A frog in a well will say there is no dragon's cave.
How can a quail know about a phoenix's nest?
When the elixir is mature, gold will naturally fill the room.
Why need to look for plants or burn reeds?


9

The essence of yin generative energy in the yang is not
     strong.
Cultivate only one aspect and it will get increasingly weak.
Tiring the body with massage and breath control is not the
     way;
Swallowing vapor and ingesting mist are crazy;

Everyone idly seeks the lead and mercury;
When will they ever see the tiger and dragon subdued?
I advise you to find the place where your body was born.
Going back to the origin and returning to the source is the
    great medicine.

### 13

If you do not know how to invert the mysterious,
How can you plant the lotus in the fire?
Lead the white tiger home and nurture it
To produce a bright pearl as round as the moon.
Relax beside the medicine furnace and watch the fires.
Let the spiritual breath follow its natural way.
When all the toxins are expelled, the elixir will be complete;
Leaping out of the cage, you will live for ten thousand
    years.

## From Part Two

### 1

First use *ch'ien* (sky) and *k'un* (earth) as your cauldron;
Then take the medicine of the raven and rabbit and cook
    them.
When these two things return to the Yellow Way,
How can the golden elixir not be liberated?

### 2

Position the furnace and set up the cauldron according to
    *ch'ien* and *k'un*.

Refine the essence of the sun and moon to stabilize the
    human spirit and soul.
Gathering and dispersing, the heated vapor is transformed.
I do not dare to talk about these mysterious wonders
    casually.


3
Stop wasting your effort at the alchemical stove.
To refine the medicine, you need to find the crescent moon
    furnace.
In there the natural true fire is born.
Who needs purple coal and bellows?


16
Take the solid center of *k'an* (water)
To change the yin in the belly of *li* (fire).
From there it is transformed into the perfect body of *ch'ien*.
To remain hidden or to fly and leap, it is all up to the mind.


17
The mercuric dragon of *chen* (thunder) comes from its
    home in *li*;
The lead tiger of *tui* (lake) is born in the position of *k'an*.
The two things come from the child giving birth to the
    mother.
Most important of all, the five elements need to enter the
    center.

### 39

If you want the valley spirit to never die,
You must rely on the mysterious female to build the
    foundation.
When the true generative energy has returned to the yellow
    golden room,
The bright pearl will never leave.

### 43

The black within the white is the mother of the elixir.
The female enclosed inside the male is the sacred fetus.
When the Great One is in the furnace, you need to guard
    it with care.
The jewels gathered in the three *tan-t'iens* (fields of energy)
    are the reflections of the three Altar Stars.

### 47

If you want to know how to refine, nourish, and circulate
    the elixir,
You need to plant the seed in your own garden.
No need to huff and puff with force and effort,
Because when the elixir is complete, it will naturally leave
    its spiritual womb.

### 54

When the medicine meets the energy, its form emerges.
Imperceptible and inaudible, the Tao merges with nature.
When the numinous pill is swallowed into the belly,

This is the first time you'll know that your destiny is not
   determined in the celestial realm.


From Part Three

   2

The internal medicine is the same as the external medicine.
When you understand the internal, you will understand the
   external.
In balancing and compounding the elixir, the substances
   are the same.
Incubation functions in two ways:
Inside there is the natural real fire
And the bright red flame in the furnace;
Outside, increasing and decreasing the heat of the external
   furnace require diligence.
Nothing is more wonderful than the true seed.


   7

The seven reverse cycles return the cinnabar to the origin;
The nine circulations return the golden nectar to the true
   reality.
Stop counting the hours from three to nine and one to nine.
However, the five elements need to be in accurate order.
Everything is dependent on the silver mercury
Flowing everywhere at all times.
When the numerics of yin and yang are met, it will
   naturally join with the spirit.
The going out and coming in are not separated from the
   mysterious female.

12

Cultivate more than eight hundred virtuous deeds;
Accumulate fully three thousand hidden merits.
Equally helping all things, friend or foe;
Only then can you do what the immortals originally did.
Tigers, rhinos, swords, and soldiers will not harm you.
You will not be drawn into the mundane mortal realm.
When the sacred writ descends, you will be ready to
    present yourself before the celestial realm,
Riding calmly on a chariot pulled by a phoenix.

### NOTES ON THE TRANSLATION

Again, there is much symbolic language here and they are
similar to those in the *Tsan-tung-chi*. As in the translation
of the *Tsan-tung-chi*, I have retained the Chinese names
*ch'ien*, *k'un*, *k'an*, and *li* for the same reasons. Again, if you
wish to know more about Taoist alchemy, you can refer to
my books *The Shambhala Guide to Taoism* and *Harmonizing
Yin and Yang: The Dragon-Tiger Classic* (forthcoming).

# 6

## *In the Playing Fields of Power*

### Taoist Magic and Sorcery

TAOIST MAGICIANS AND SORCERERS ARE "artists of power." They are individuals who have penetrated the mysteries of the Tao and have entered into an intimate relationship with both the natural and supernatural forces. Standing between ordinary reality and the subtle world of spirits, deities, and the natural elements, they give us a glimpse of the power of the Tao that we are normally unaware of in our everyday lives.

### *Stories of Taoist Immortals, Magicians, and Sorcerers*

Stories of Taoist immortals, magicians, and sorcerers are very much a part of Chinese culture. When I was growing up in Hong Kong, my grandmother and my aunt told me many such stories.

The story of Tung-fang Shuo (The Seeker in the East) is based on the *Shen-hsien chuan* (Biographies of the Immortals) and the legends of Emperor Wu-ti of the Western Han dynasty (206 BCE–8 CE). The story of Chang Tao-ling, the founder of the Celestial Teachers sect and the father of devotional Taoism, is reconstructed from the *Shen-hsien chuan*, popular stories, and a Chinese opera script.

As you read the stories, you will notice that Taoist immortals are individuals who are endowed with both wisdom and power. Many Taoist immortals were magicians, diviners, and sorcerers, and possessed the same skills as the shamans did in the prehistoric times.

## Tung-fang Shuo (Seeker in the East)

When Tung-fang Shuo was a boy, he once left home and did not return until a year later. His family was worried, and when he came home, his brother said, "Where have you been? You were away for almost a year."

Tung-fang Shuo replied, "I was playing on the beach and got sprayed by the salt water. So I went to the Deep Spring to wash the salt off my clothes. I left home early in the morning, and it's only lunchtime now. Why do you say that I've been away for a year?"

His brother exclaimed, "The Deep Spring is ten thousand miles from here! It would take a normal person more than a year to get there and back. You must be joking!"

When Tung-fang Shuo was twenty-two years old, he wrote a letter to Wu-ti, the Han emperor. In the letter he said, "I was orphaned at an early age and was brought up

*Tung-fang Shuo washing in the Deep Spring.*

by my brother. I mastered the classics when I was twelve. At fifteen I became an expert in the martial arts. At sixteen I became a master poet and memorized twenty thousand lines of song. At nineteen I mastered the science of warfare and the art of diplomacy. Now, at twenty-two, I stand head and shoulders above everyone. My body is strong and grace-ful. My mind is agile and cunning. I am honest and trust-worthy, brave and honorable. I am someone whom your majesty should have in your service!"

Many people would have been offended by Tung-fang Shuo's manner of presenting himself, but the emperor saw that Tung-fang Shuo was no ordinary person. He not only employed the young man in his service but made Tung-fang Shuo his personal advisor.

The emperor valued Tung-fang Shuo's friendship and lavished him with gifts. He even sent Tung-fang Shuo a beautiful woman to be his wife. However, every time the emperor sent gifts of silks and gold to his friend, Tung-fang Shuo turned all the gifts over to his wife. People made fun of his strange behavior and joked, "Either he really loves his wife or he is afraid of her!" But Tung-fang Shuo was not offended. He only laughed and said, "I am a hermit who escapes worldly matters by hiding in the palace!"

Often Tung-fang Shuo would get drunk and sing in a loud voice:

The world is too muddy,
Therefore I hide behind the gates of the Palace.
The Palace is a place where I can cultivate my life,
Why do I need to be a hermit in the deep mountains?

Before Tung-fang Shuo was about to leave the mortal realm, he made a remark to the emperor, "No one knows where I came from and where I will go. Only the astronomer who keeps a record of the stars knows about my true identity."

One day, Tung-fang Shuo was nowhere to be seen. The emperor was worried about his friend. Suddenly, remembering what Tung-fang Shuo had said a few days previously, he summoned the court astronomer and asked about Tung-fang Shuo.

The court astronomer was bewildered. He said, "Your majesty, I honestly do not know Tung-fang Shuo's true identity."

The emperor was a very clever man. He sensed that Tung-fang Shuo's identity must be related to the patterns of stars in the sky. Otherwise, he would not have mentioned that only the keeper of the record of the stars would know his identity.

Turning to the astronomer, the emperor asked, "In your observation of the stars in the last forty years, did you notice anything out of the ordinary?"

The astronomer replied, "My lord, I did notice that forty years ago a star mysteriously disappeared and then a few days ago reappeared again."

The emperor finally understood. He sighed and said, "In the eighteen years that Tung-fang Shuo was with me, I did not even know that he was a sky immortal. What a pity!"

## *Chang Tao-ling (The Celestial Teacher)*

Chang Tao-ling stood over seven feet tall and had bushy eyebrows, a large round forehead, and a hawk-beak nose. On the sole of his right foot were seven black dots arranged in the pattern of the seven stars of the Northern Bushel (Big Dipper). He had long, powerful arms that came down to his knees, and he walked with a gait that had the strength of the tiger and the speed of the dragon.

Just before Chang Tao-ling was conceived, his mother dreamed that she saw a giant descending from the North Pole Star. The lord of the North Star came toward her and gave her a flower. When she awoke the next morning, she smelled wisps of fragrance in her room and discovered that she had conceived a child. The fragrance lasted throughout the ten months while she carried the baby in her womb.

On the day Chang Tao-ling was born, a yellow cloud covered the house and purple mist hovered about his mother's bedchamber. When he came out of his mother's womb, music and fragrance filled the air, and the room was flooded with light that matched the brilliance of the sun and moon.

Chang Tao-ling was exceptionally intelligent. At seven he understood the teachings of Lao-tzu's *Tao-te ching*. By twelve he had mastered the *I-ching* and the classics of divination. As a young man, Chang Tao-ling served his community as a provincial administrator but he continued to study the arts of the Tao.

One day, while he was meditating in his retreat, a white

tiger came to his side. In its mouth was a scroll of sacred scripture. Chang Tao-ling knew that it was time for him to leave the world of politics to pursue the Tao.

He resigned his position of civil administrator and became a hermit in the mountains. When the emperor heard about Chang Tao-ling's retirement, he offered him the title Imperial Teacher and begged him to return to the service of the government. Three times the emperor invited him, and each time Chang Tao-ling refused.

When Chang Tao-ling realized that he would not be left in peace, he moved to the remote and mountainous region of Szechuan. There where the streams ran deep and the waterfalls cascaded down precipitous cliffs, Chang Tao-ling selected a cave where he could meditate, learn the arts of immortality, and attain the Tao.

Chang Tao-ling stayed in his cave for many years until one day he heard the cry of a white crane. He knew it was a sign that he would attain enlightenment soon. A year later, when Chang Tao-ling was stoking the fires of the furnace to incubate the Dragon-Tiger Elixir, a red shaft of light appeared and illuminated the cavern. Another year later, a white tiger and a green dragon came into the cave and sat by the side of the cauldron to protect the elixir. Finally, three years after Chang Tao-ling had heard the call of the white crane, the elixir was completed and Chang Tao-ling became an immortal.

Chang Tao-ling left his cave and traveled throughout the river valleys and mountains of Szechuan. On one of his journeys he met Lao-tzu, who taught him how to fly to the stars and tunnel under the earth. When Lao-tzu departed, he gave Chang Tao-ling a scroll of talismans that had the power to heal the sick and a magic sword that could drive away malevolent spirits.

As time went on, Chang Tao-ling's skill in the arts of sorcery matured. Soon he could make himself invisible or change himself into any shape he wished. He could hear and see over great distances and could call down rain and snow. He could heal the sick and drive away evil spirits. His fame spread far and wide, and people called him the Celestial Teacher, for they believed that he was an immortal from the celestial realm.

One time, six evil spirits were wreaking havoc in Szechuan. Lao-tzu appeared to Chang Tao-ling and told him to return to Szechuan to capture the spirits and bring them to judgment. Chang Tao-ling secluded himself for one thousand days to prepare for this encounter.

When the six lords of evil heard that Chang Tao-ling was preparing to fight them, they gathered a large army of ghosts, ghouls, zombies, and other evil creatures. Meanwhile, Chang Tao-ling also made his preparations. He selected a green mound outside the city of Cheng-tu and built a tower with an altar in the middle. On the altar he placed objects of power, such as magical mirrors, bells, and talismans.

At the hour of *tzu* (11:00 P.M.) Chang Tao-ling ascended the tower and invoked the wind, rain, and thunder to beat upon the army of the evil spirits. Chang Tao-ling also drew talismans of power and called on the celestial deities to fight the evil forces. The lords of evil sent flaming spears and arrows to hit Chang Tao-ling, but none of them could harm him. As the spears and arrows came toward him, Chang Tao-ling waved his sword of power, and the weapons were transformed into lotus flowers.

The lords of evil then sent an army of hungry ghosts to attack Chang Tao-ling, but when they reached the altar, Chang Tao-ling drew a talisman, and all the ghosts fell on their knees and begged for compassion. Then the lords of evil sent an army of ghouls, vampires, and zombies to attack Chang Tao-ling. When these creatures came near the altar, Chang Tao-ling rang his magical bells, and the undead clutched their ears and fell to the ground, never to rise again.

Seeing that their minions had failed, the six lords of evil came forward themselves to attack Chang Tao-ling. Chang Tao-ling grasped his sword and drew the Great Seal of Power. The sword emitted a stream of bright light, which was transformed into a net. The net descended onto the six evil spirits and formed a cage around them. When the six lords of evil saw Chang Tao-ling striding toward them with his sword of power, they begged for mercy and forgiveness. Chang Tao-ling said to them, "You have brought illness and suffering to many people, and for these evil deeds you must be punished. But, as the Celestial Way is compassionate, I shall not kill you. I shall, however, punish you by keeping you locked inside the depths of a mountain. In this way you will not harm people again."

When the people saw that the six lords of evil were captured by Chang Tao-ling, they came to thank him and asked him to teach them his magic. Chang Tao-ling did not want to turn them away, so he told them to organize themselves into groups to help people who were in need. He also told the people that the most effective way to fight evil was to do good deeds. If everyone did only what was good, evil could not take hold.

To his close followers, Chang Tao-ling taught the magic of talismans and told them to always use the power of sorcery for good and never for evil. On the day he ascended to the celestial realm, he left the sword of power and the Great Seal to his son and entrusted him to teach and lead the followers of the Celestial Teachers' Way.

### Feng-shen Yen-yi (*Investiture of the Gods*)

The *Feng-shen yen-yi* was written in the Ming dynasty (1368–1644 CE) by novelist and Taoist practitioner Lu Hsi-hsing. The book is a fantasy novel set against the background of the fall of the Shang dynasty (1766–1121 BCE) and the founding of the Chou dynasty (1122–221 BCE). Like its more famous contemporary works *Journey to the West* and *Heroes of the Marsh*, it depicts the classic struggle of good against evil and the triumph of the good at the end.

The cast of characters in the *Feng-shen yen-yi* includes folk deities, Taoist immortals, Buddhist arhats, nature spirits, animal spirits, shamans, sorcerers, superheroes, kings, princes, ministers, and commoners. As the novel says,

"Everyone in the world was involved in this gigantic struggle; few did not take sides."

The following excerpt describes how Kiang Tzu-ya, a Taoist sorcerer and chief advisor to the duke of Chou (later King Wen, the first emperor of the Chou dynasty), used his magical powers to summon the elements to defeat the army of the evil king of Shang.

## Kiang Tzu-ya Summons the Elements

Tzu-ya instructed his assistant to build a mound about three feet high. When it was completed, Tzu-ya climbed to the top of the mound and undid the knot in his hair. With a sword in his hand, he faced east toward the direction of the Kun-lun Mountains, and prostrated. Then he walked the steps of the Big Dipper and began his magic ritual, uttering incantations and scattering talismanic water.

Soon, a strong wind blew and whistled through the forest. Dust churned up from the ground and nothing could be seen. The sky darkened and the earth rumbled. In the distance, the waves crashed onto the shore and the mountains shook. Bells and chimes on the prayer flags clanged against each other. All who stood nearby were unable to open their eyes.

Far away, in the enemy camp, the weather was warm and there were only small gusts of wind. The commanding generals said among themselves, "This is a good sign. Even the weather is on our side. Our emperor has the favor of the celestial lords, for they have sent this refreshing wind to cool us on our march."

However, as the armies of the evil emperor approached Tzu-ya's camp, the situation changed. Tzu-ya summoned a cold wind, and for three days it blew continuously. The imperial soldiers began to whisper to each other, "We are living in unfortunate times. It is said that the weather will become unpredictable when there are problems in the country."

An hour later, a few snowflakes fluttered around. The imperial soldiers began to complain, "We are dressed in summer uniforms. How can we survive in this cold?"

Not long after that, the snow became heavy, and the soldiers could hardly see what was in front of them. Now and then, they could hear avalanches crashing down the mountain slopes. The land became a wall of pure white. Wolves howled, their cries coming out of nowhere. The snow soon became ankle-deep, then knee-deep. The progress of the imperial army came to a halt.

The commanding general looked at his lieutenants and said, "I have never seen snow this heavy in the middle of summer." The general, an old man, was having a hard time enduring the cold. All the soldiers were huddled in heaps, stricken with cold. There was nothing that their commanders could do to keep them moving.

Meanwhile, in Tzu-ya's camp, everyone was prepared for the snow. The soldiers stood in their ranks, grateful that they were wearing padded jackets and straw hats. Everyone was awed by Tzu-ya's power.

Tzu-ya then asked his assistant, "How deep is the snow?"

The young man replied, "In the higher places it is about two feet, but in the valleys the drifts must be at least four or five feet."

Tzu-ya returned to the mound, undid the topknot from his hair, drew talismans in the air with his sword, and chanted. At once, the snow clouds disappeared and a bright sun shone. The ice and snow melted and a torrent of water rushed down the mountain sides into the valley. Just when the water has formed a lake in the valley, Tzu-ya changed his incantations. He drew another talisman and whipped up a cold wind. The sun disappeared behind ominous black clouds and the water froze immediately.

When Tzu-ya looked at the direction where the imperial army was stranded, he saw broken flags and banners. Turning to his assistant he said, "Lead twenty strong men into the enemy camp and capture the commanders."

# 7

## The Tao in Everyday Life

TAOIST ETHICS

ALTHOUGH ENLIGHTENMENT AND THE attainment of immortality are the highest goals of Taoism, the importance of everyday living in the mortal world is not neglected in Taoist practice. After all, it is in our mortal lifetime that we prepare ourselves for the return to the Tao. Taoist ethics are intimately tied to traditional Chinese views of right action. Walking in the "ways of goodness" will ensure that we will live a peaceful, prosperous, healthy, and long life. It is also a responsibility that every human being should have during his or her lifetime in the mortal realm.

### Chih-sun-tzu chung-chieh ching
(*Master Red Pine's Book of Discipline*)

The *Chih-sun tzu chung-chieh ching* was written during the Six Dynasties (between the fifth and sixth centuries CE). The text uses a conversation between the Yellow Emperor and the sage Master Red Pine to present the ethics of right thinking and right action. In Taoist legend, Master Red Pine was a shaman and rainmaker during the time of the Yellow Emperor. A teacher of humanity, Master Red Pine has appeared from time to time to teach mortals.

## *From the* Chih-sun tzu chung-chieh ching

The Yellow Emperor bowed and addressed Chih-sun Tzu, "I see tens of thousands of people born, each person having a different destiny. Some are rich and some are poor; some live a long life and some die young. Some spend their lives in prison locked up in chains; some are plagued with illness; some die suddenly without becoming ill; and some enjoy longevity and prosperity. Please explain to me why there is such inequality in people's fortunes?"

Chih-sun Tzu said, "Everyone is born under the guardianship of stars. Some stars have great influence over our lives and some have less influence. These stars determine whether someone will be born as a human or animal, whether the individual will live long or die young, whether he or she will rise or fall in fortune, be rich or poor, and live or die. Those who do charitable deeds will be blessed with the spirit of goodness. Fortune and virtue will follow them. Evil will not come near them. The spirits will protect them. People will respect them. Disaster will not befall them. Those who do bad deeds will be visited by the spirit of evil. Misfortune will follow them. Blessings will leave them. The baleful stars will shine on them. People will hate them. Disasters will gather around them.

"In our everyday life, if we think and act against the sky and the earth, punishment will not come lightly. If we do bad deeds, the spirit in us will report to the stars and our longevity will be decreased. The celestial vapor will leave and the terrestrial vapor will suffocate us. This is what it means to meet with misfortune."

The Yellow Emperor then asked, "How long can humans live?"

Chih-sun Tzu replied, "When we tumble out of our mother's womb onto the ground, the celestial lords gave us a life span of forty-three thousand and eight hundred days. This comes to one hundred and twenty years. There is one birthday each year. Thus, humans are given a chance to experience one hundred and twenty birthdays. Those who have broken the laws of the sky and the earth will have birthdays taken from them or will have their lives terminated."

The Yellow Emperor asked again, "How about those who return to the celestial realm in their mother's womb, or those who die in infancy? These people did not have the chance to commit wrongdoings. How could they have offended the sky and earth?"

Chih-sun Tzu said, "When ancestors have done bad deeds, retribution will be carried over to their descendants. This is why the ancient sages have left their teachings in the sacred scriptures to advise people to do good deeds and know what is evil. In this way their children and grandchildren will reap the benefits of fortune.

"Humanity is born in the midst of the sky and earth and is the product of the vapor of yin and yang. The sky is high but it responds to what happens below. The earth is humble but it elicits responses from the sky. Without a word, the sky moves the four seasons. Without a word, the earth creates the ten thousand things and humanity. When our emotions and desires are stirred, the powers in the sky and the earth will know it. Therefore it is said that the celestial realm knows four things. It knows who complains and who is ungrateful to the earth and the sky. When the sky gave us life, *ch'ien* and *k'un* are in our father and mother, the sun and moon are in our eyes, and the stars are in our cavities. Movement of wind and the strength of fire give us the warm vapor of life. When we die, we return to the earth.

"In the sky the Three Altars Stars, the Northern Bushel, and the Pole Star govern longevity and prosperity. The T'ai-i star is situated on top of the head. It monitors our actions and takes away our longevity if we do bad deeds. If one year of life is taken, the star on top of the head will become dim. The individual will feel weak and be plagued with small illnesses. If ten years are taken away, parts of the star will gradually disappear, and the individual will always be ill. If twenty years are taken away, the light of the star will be damaged beyond repair, and the individual will be bedridden permanently or be imprisoned. If thirty years are taken away, the star will disintegrate and fall from the sky like a shooting star. Not only will the individual die before his or her time, but the punishment will carry over to the descendants until the family line is extinguished.

"People do not know that they have committed wrongdoings. They only say that their lives are short. The sky does not deceive. It shows us omens day and night—in the moon and sun, in thunder and lightning, in snow and in rainbows, in the eclipses of the sun and moon, and in the shooting stars. These phenomena all carry messages from the celestial realm. Earth does not deceive us either. Its response affects all things. Floods, landslides, earthquakes, ferocious winds, tornadoes, locusts, drought, famine, and poisonous gas are all messages from earth. The spirits do not deceive. Fortune and misfortune, disaster and blessing, are their messages. The ruler of the country cannot deceive us. Signs from the stars, disasters and destruction in the world, the people's loyalty—all these events tell us about the ruler.

"People's action, speech, and intention elicit responses from the sky and the earth. The sages tell us that the great sky follows virtue and does not favor anyone. Therefore we should heed its warnings and those of the great ones and the sages. The celestial lords know who has done good deeds and who has done bad ones. People cannot hide acts of murder, for the spirits of the underworld can see into their hearts and intention. When people have committed a hundred wrongs, the spirits of the underworld will drink their essence. If they have committed a thousand wrongs, earth will take away their human form and bind them with chains. This is retribution from both the yin and yang domains. The celestial realm has established a set of rules and ethics. If people break these rules, the deities, the spirits of the underworld, and the powers of the sky and earth will punish them."

The Yellow Emperor then asked, "Can you tell me more about how the immortals view good and evil, and how fortune and blessings are given?"

Chih-sun-tzu replied, "Practice daily the methods of cultivating your body, your life, and your inner nature. Do good deeds, and always think and act in kindness. If you stay away from three acts of evil every day, then within three years, the celestial lords will send the stars of fortune to visit you, and you will be rewarded with fortune. If you do bad deeds, think evil things, and teach others evil ways, within three years, disaster will come to you. You will lose your health, your wealth, and you will die.

"When harmful vapor spreads on earth, things will go badly for people. The appearance of ugly, evil things in the sky is the result of the nine wrongs on earth. Thus, it is said that the cure for evil is goodness, and evil is the bane of the good. Those who are kind should be the teachers of those who are evil. The presence of evil in the world tells us that we need more people who are good. The existence of blessing means that retribution is thwarted by acts of goodness. On the other hand, retribution is what remains of evil after goodness has been accounted for.

"Sometimes good people meet with disaster. This is because retribution was handed down to them by their ancestors. Those who do good deeds do not need to pick auspicious days for special events. Whenever good deeds are done, there will be blessings even in the midst of disaster. The hundred spirits and guardian deities will make sure that misfortune does not occur. However, for those who do evil deeds all their lives, even if they pick auspicious days for special events, there will be disaster on the days of blessing. The evil spirits will harm them. The spirits who give blessings will avoid them. If people do charitable deeds frequently, the celestial lords will naturally reward them with prosperity and longevity. The relationship between good deeds and rewards is like the effect of a thing on its shadow. Therefore, if you do not want to meet with misfortune or harm, you must not offend the sky and the earth. You must know how to cultivate yourself and affect your destiny."

# 8

## *Encountering the Sacred*

THE TAOIST CEREMONIES

I N SPIRITUAL TRADITIONS, CEREMONIES
create a sacred time and space for humanity to meet
the powers of the universe. Many Taoist ceremonies
are rooted in ancient Chinese rites that predate the emer-
gence of Taoism as a philosophy and a spiritual tradition.
However, they are also enriched by two thousand years of
Taoist spiritual practice.

All Taoist ceremonies are preceded by purification rituals that prepare the ceremonial grounds and the participants for the event. The first selections in this chapter, the
Fa-lu Chants, are recited by participants before the main
part of a ceremony is performed. The second selection,
from the *Chai-chieh lu* (Correct Procedures of Purification
and Preparation for Festival Services), describes the kinds
of purification rites that accompany the Taoist ceremonies.

### *The Fa-lu (Lighting the Stove) Chants*

The Fa-lu Chants are invocations recited at the beginning
of a liturgy. They are used to induce the participants into

the appropriate state of mind and remind them of the purpose and meaning of the ceremony—to bring humanity closer to the Tao.

Before the main body of a liturgy is chanted or a ceremony is performed, the ceremonial grounds (temple, shrine, and altar) and the hearts, minds, and bodies of the participants must be purified. The purification rituals and the chanting are a covenant made between humanity and the celestial deities, who are guardians of the Tao. As people make a solemn promise to purify themselves and to embrace the principles of the Tao, the deities renew their promise to protect, guide, and teach. Together, the sacred powers and humanity ensure that the universe is forever filled with the life-giving breath of the Tao.

## Lighting the Stove

The smoke rises from the stove.
The breath of the Tao lingers.
With dedication I offer this fragrant incense.
Let its scent surround the universe.
Let it spread to the ten directions.
Let all the spirits reveal their golden light.

## Dedication of Incense

The Tao is approached from the heart.
As the smoke rises, let my heart ascend to the Tao.
Before the fragrant incense and jade pure stove,
I stand single-minded before the celestial lords.
Let the true spirit descend.
Let the immortals come.
This I sincerely petition.
Let my vision reach the nine celestial realms.

## Purification of the Mind

The stars of the Great Altar constellation
Are forever rotating and changing.
They save us from evil and disaster;
They protect us and guard our bodies.
Let my thoughts be intelligent and pure.
Let my heart's spirit be peaceful and calm.
Let my three souls live forever.
Let the spirit-soul never stray from me.

## Purification of the Mouth

May the guardian jewel of speech
Expel the impure air in us.
May the guardian of our tongue
Direct us to say what is upright.
Let our health be enhanced,
And let the spirit be cultivated.
May the guardian of our teeth
Help us to retain the good and reject the evil.
May the guardian of the throat let out the tiger's roar.
May the guardian of vital energy nourish the sweet nectar.
May the guardian of the mind hasten the completion of the
    golden elixir,
And help us to understand the mystery of the origin.
May the guardian of thought cultivate the sweet saliva,
So that the breath of the Tao will stay with me forever.


## Purification of the Body

Every day I cleanse my body.
Watching the moon I cultivate my form.
The immortals lift me up.
The fair lady hovers over my being.
The twenty-eight constellations
Are united with me.
The Celestial Lord Ling-pao

Protects my soul.
He guards the spirit and soul of sentient beings,
And ensures that the internal organs are bright and whole.
Let the Green Dragon and the White Tiger
Array their power around me.
Let the Red Raven and the Black Tortoise
Protect my true spirit.

## Purification of the Sky and the Earth

When sky and earth follow the natural way,
The impure breath will disappear.
The mysterious emptiness of the cavern
Will illuminate the great oneness.
May the powerful spirits of the eight directions
Guide me to follow the natural course.
May the Celestial Lord Ling-pao protect my life.
Let my petitions reach the nine levels of the sky.
Let the guardians of the celestial realms
And the ancient mystery of the great cavern
Smite the evil spirits, bind the unlawful beings,
And destroy the ten thousand monsters.
The sacred writ of the central mountain,
Is the jade word from the great beginning.
Chant this once,
And the monsters will flee and life will be preserved.
Do this systematically in the five mountains.
Let it be heard across the eight seas.

The demon lord will be unable to move,
And the internal domain will be guarded.
The forces of destruction will be dispersed,
And the Breath of the Tao will exist forever.

## Revealing the Golden Light

The great mysterious origin of the sky and earth,
Is the root of the ten thousand breaths.
It gives me life, saves me from a million retributions,
And instructs me in the ways of the spirit.
Inside and outside the three realms
Only the Tao is supreme.
Its essence emanates a golden light.
It covers my body;
It cannot be seen;
It cannot be heard;
It embodies the sky and the earth;
And nourishes and teaches all sentient beings.
Chant it ten thousand times,
And the body will glow with light.
The guardians of the three realms will watch over me;
The five emperors will welcome me;
The ten thousand spirits will prostrate before me;
And the thunder lord will bend to my will.
Ghosts and evil spirits will lose their courage;
Evil nymphs and creatures will lose their shape.
Rumblings are heard within,

As voice of the spirit of thunder resonates.
As copulation occurs in the cavern,
The five vapors fill the air.
Let the golden light quickly appear
To protect the enlightened being.

## Chai-chieh lu (*Correct Procedures of Purification and Preparation for Festival Services*)

The *Chai-chieh lu* is a collection of purification rites (*chai*) and proper codes (*chieh*) of behavior required of Taoists participating in sacred ceremonies. Its anonymous author was most likely a Taoist priest of the T'ang dynasty (618–906 CE).

The excerpts below are taken from four sections in the *Chai-chieh lu*. The Introductory section discusses the nature of purification and the meaning of *chai*. In Taoist practice, *chai* is the rite of purification that cleanses the ceremonial grounds and prepares the participants for the sacred festivals.

The excerpt from the section "The Six Tung-hsüan Lingpao Purifications and Ten Vows" describes ten Taoist vows of discipline and six types of purification rites. It is interesting that in addition to ethical behaviors such as compassion for others and abstinence from killing and stealing, one of the ten vows calls for conserving water and planting trees. This ecological ethic is quite remarkable. It shows that in Taoist spirituality, the respect for nature is never far away.

The excerpt from "The Six Kinds of Chai" describes six purification rites associated with six kinds of sacred ceremonies. Note that the Shang-ch'ing Purification mentioned here is not associated with specific rituals or ceremonies of Shang-ch'ing Taoism, the mystical sect that emerged in the third and fourth centuries. Rather, they refer to general purification rites observed in the preparation of all sacred ceremonies.

In the last excerpt, "The Nine Diets of Purification," the reader is given a feel for what the Taoist dietary regulations are like. They range from a diet of millet and grains to feeding on the Breath of the Tao. Each diet is associated with a level of spiritual development, and practitioners are advised to follow a certain diet only when they are ready. Even so, only the few who have reached the highest levels of spiritual attainment observe the rites of purification every day.

## *From the* Chai-chieh lu

### FROM THE INTRODUCTION

There are three kinds of *chai*, or purifications. In the first kind of purification, offerings are made to atone for wrongdoings and to accumulate merits. The second kind of purification is fasting or abstaining from rich foods. It clears the mind, cleanses the body, and prepares the participants for the sacred ceremonies. This rite can be performed by individuals who take the Middle Path [the path of performing the sacred ceremonies]. The third kind of purification is emptying the mind of desire. It purifies the spirit and dissolves negative attitudes. It cultivates wisdom and curbs anxiety. When there are no thoughts, one will turn to the Tao. When there is no desire or craving, one will be content. When there are no negative attitudes and no scheming, the mind is centered and is at one with the Tao.

## THE SIX TUNG-HSÜAN LING-PAO (PRECIOUS JEWELS OF THE MYSTERIOUS CAVERN) PURIFICATIONS AND TEN VOWS

There are five abstinences in the Taoist religion. First, do not kill. Second, do not get intoxicated. Third, do not speak falsely. Fourth, do not steal. Fifth, do not indulge in sensual pleasure. There are ten ways of goodness. First, honor your parents. Second, be dedicated in everything you do. Third, be kind and compassionate to all things. Fourth, be tolerant and forgiving. Fifth, speak out against things that are wrong. Sixth, be selfless and help others. Seventh, value the life of all sentient beings and respect nature. Eighth, help conserve water, plant trees, and build bridges. Ninth, always think of the welfare of others. Tenth, recite the scriptures of the Three Treasures, keep the vows, and make offerings of incense and flowers. An individual who observes the five abstinences and follows the ten good ways will be protected by the celestial spirits. Remember, good things are planted by your actions.

## THE SIX KINDS OF CHAI
## (PURIFICATIONS FOR CEREMONIES)

The *Ti-yi tao-men ta-lun* (The Great Book of the Practices of Taoism) states that there are three rites of Shang-
ch'ing purification. First, the participants must spend time
in solitude, eat without company, reduce activity to slow
the breath, and cleanse the body. Second, the altars must
be purified in a solemn manner. Third, the participants
must calm their emotions and clear the mind of desire and
negative thoughts.

There are six rites of Ling-pao purifications. The first,
the Golden Register Purification rites, are used for petitions
made on behalf of the nation. The second, the Yellow Register Purification rites, are for petitions asking for deliverance
from suffering. The third set of Ling-pao purification rites,
called Understanding the Truth, is for ceremonies of repen-
tance made on behalf of the dead. The fourth is the Three
Agents Purification rite, and it is used to petition the Lords
of the Three Realms (Sky, Earth, and Water) for forgiveness. The fifth is the Eight Festival Purification rite, and it
is used to ask for forgiveness of past wrongdoings. The sixth
is the Common Purification rite, and it is used for ceremonies of intercession on behalf of the common citizen.

The Tung-shen (Cavern Spirit) Purification rite is a short
ritual used to cleanse the ceremonial ground of worldly
dust and prepare it for visits from the spirits.

The T'ai-i (Ancient Beginning) Purification rite is used
for solemn and stately occasions.

There is also a purification rite that prepares individuals for receiving instruction. These rites emphasize simplicity and humility.

The rite of purification through suffering emphasizes hard work and service to others.

## THE NINE DIETS OF PURIFICATION

The *Hsüan-men ta-lun* (Great Discourse on Taoist Practices) states that there are nine diets of purification.

The first is a diet of grain, the second vegetarianism, the third fasting, the fourth eating the essence of energy, the fifth eating yellow sprouts, the sixth swallowing light, the seventh ingesting vapor and mist, the eighth absorbing the primordial vapor, and the ninth feeding like a fetus in the womb.

A diet of grain consists of millet and wheat. Vegetarianism is a diet of leafy vegetables and fungus. Fasting is abstaining from eating. Eating the essence of energy is drinking talismanic water and ingesting minerals. Eating yellow sprouts means absorbing the essence of the clouds. Swallowing light is swallowing the light of the sun, moon, and Northern Bushel (Big Dipper) stars. Eating vapor and mist is absorbing the vapor of the Great Harmony from the four directions. Eating the primordial vapor is absorbing the vapor of the three celestial realms and the essence of the Great Harmony from the Great Void. To feed like a fetus is to be nourished by the original essence that was present at conception and be nurtured by the pristine energy that envelops the fetus in the womb.

# 9

## *The Arts of Longevity*

### Cultivating the Mind

P RACTITIONERS OF TAOIST SPIRITUALITY use meditation as the primary method to cultivate the mind for health, longevity, and spiritual transformation.

The translations in this section are chosen to give the reader a feel for the different kinds of Taoist meditation. Please do not use them as meditation manuals. The practice of Taoist meditation requires formal instruction and supervision from a qualified teacher. Unguided practice can lead to injuries, and the author and publisher are not responsible for any complications that result from using these texts as manuals.

**Shang-ch'ing t'ai-shang ti-chün chiu-chen chung-ching**
(*Scripture of the High Pure Realm's Highest Celestial Lord's Nine True Forms*)

This text describes a form of meditation that was practiced by the Shang-ch'ing mystics. According to Shang-ch'ing

Taoism, this meditation manual was transmitted by the Immortal Chih-sun-tzu (Master Red Pine) to the Shang-ch'ing patriarch and immortal Chou-chün (the Lord Chou).

The text describes the procedures for visualizing the nine true forms of the Lord of the High Pure Realm. The goal of Shang-ch'ing meditation is to keep the guardian deities within by visualizing them and holding onto their images. If the guardians stay within the body, health and longevity are assured. If the guardians leave, the practitioner will become ill or even die.

# *From* Shang-ch'ing t'ai-shang ti-chün chiu-chen chung-ching

### From "Method of the First True Form"

Slow the breath, close the eyes, and visualize the image of the Lord of Celestial Essence sitting in your heart. He is called the Great Spirit. Next, visualize a purple vapor coming from the mouth of the Great Spirit spreading outward from the heart. The vapor ascends like a straight pole to the *ni-wan* (Mud Ball) cavity in the head.

### From "Method of the Second True Form"

In your mind visualize the image of the Lord of the Jade Stone sending a pearl into your throat down to the stomach. The pearl is transformed into a white vapor that spreads to the hundred joints. Next, visualize a white vapor coming out of the mouth of the Great Spirit to hover around your bones. The vapor floats around the nine external and internal levels like clouds, mist, and smoke.

## From "Method of the Third True Form"

Go into your room, clasp your hands together, and put them on your crossed legs. Slow the breath, close your eyes, and visualize the Lord of the Original Beginning floating around in the bloodstream and the generative fluids in the body. Next, visualize a yellow vapor coming out his mouth to wrap around all the openings in the nine levels, so that there is no separation between the internal and external environment.

## From "Method of the Fourth True Form"

Go into your room, clasp your hands together, and put them on your crossed legs. Slow down the breath, close your eyes, and visualize the Bright and Clear Great Lord entering to sit inside the liver. Next, visualize a blue vapor coming out of his mouth to fill the liver and the nine levels.

## From "Method of the Fifth True Form"

Go into your room, clasp your hands together, and put them on your crossed legs. Slow down the breath, close your eyes, and visualize, keeping in your mind the image of the Bright Lord entering the spleen. Next, visualize a green vapor coming out of his mouth to fill the spleen. Let the vapor rise up the nine levels into the *ni-wan* cavity, where it hovers and vibrates inside and outside the grotto.

## From "Method of the Sixth True Form"

Go into your room, clasp your hands together, and put them on your legs. Slow down the breath, close your eyes, and visualize the Lord of the Upper Realm, named Primal Jade, entering to sit in the lungs. Next, visualize a vapor of five colors coming from his mouth, to fill the lungs and ascending the nine levels to the *ni-wan* cavity where it hovers around inside and outside.

## From "Method of the Seventh True Form"

Go into your room, clasp your hands together, and put them on your legs. Slow down the breath, close your eyes, and visualize the image of the Lord of the Mysterious Yang entering the two kidneys. Next, visualize a red vapor coming out of his mouth filling the kidneys and rising up the nine levels into the *ni-wan* cavity, where it hovers around inside and outside.

## From "Method of the Eighth True Form"

Go into your room, clasp your hands together, and put them on your legs. Slow down the breath, close your eyes, and visualize the Lord of the Internal Environment entering to sit in the gallbladder. Next, visualize a vapor of five colors coming out of his mouth to fill the gallbladder and rising up the nine levels into the *ni-wan* cavity, where it hovers inside and outside like clouds and mist.

## From "Method of the Ninth True Form"

Go into your room, clasp your hands together, and put them on your legs. Slow down the breath, close your eyes, and visualize the Lord High Emperor inside the purple chamber of the *ni-wan* cavity. Next, visualize a purple vapor filling the mouth and rising through the nine levels. Then visualize the purple vapor coming out of his mouth to hover around your teeth before rising through the nine levels. This vapor circulates in the body thirty-six times, floating and vibrating as if the sun were inside.

### NOTES ON THE TRANSLATION

The *ni-wan* cavity is in the forehead and is the meeting point of many energy pathways. It is also the point where the spirit is gathered, nurtured, and liberated. In Shang-ch'ing practice, the *ni-wan* is the location where the spirit leaves and reenters the body after its journey to the other realms.

The nine levels are technically known as the Nine Levels of the Celestial Domain. They are the nine chambers inside the head that the vapor or internal energy must penetrate before it can reach the *ni-wan* cavity.

Tung-hsüan ling-pao ting-kuan ching (*The Mysterious Grotto Sacred Spirit Scripture on Concentrated Observation*)

This is a treatise on the form of Taoist meditation known as Concentrated Observation (*ting-kuan*) or Internal Observation (*nei-kuan*). The method calls for stilling the mind, eradicating thoughts, and becoming nonattached to the outside world. Written in the Sung dynasty, this text shows the influence of T'ien-tai Buddhism, especially the meditation practiced by this Buddhist sect.

According to the theory of Concentrated Observation, all things originate from the activity of the mind. Therefore, by stopping thinking, the practitioners will come to realize that all things are empty. In emptiness, illusions are dissolved and the underlying reality of the Tao is experienced.

Despite the Buddhist influence, Taoist *ting-kuan* meditation is not identical to Buddhist insight meditation. When you read the text below, you will notice that this form of Taoist meditation goes beyond stilling the mind. It uses *vipassana* (insight) and T'ien-tai techniques to build the initial foundations, but in the higher levels, the practitioner undergoes transformations in body and mind that are alchemical in nature. The realization that all things are empty is only the first step in the transformation of the body to vapor, the vapor to spirit, and the union of the spirit with the Tao.

The *Tung-hsüan ling-pao ting-kuan ching* is translated in full below. When you read the text, notice the absence of visualization and mantras and the emphasis on emptying the mind. The practitioner does not focus on any part of the body, nor is he or she required to adopt specific body postures while meditating.

## Tung-hsüan ling-pao ting-kuan ching

The Celestial Lord said to Immortal Tso-hsüan:

If you want to cultivate the Tao, you must let go of worldly things. Disconnect yourself from everything in the outside world so that nothing will disturb your mind. Then you can practice meditation in peace.

Quiet observation begins in the mind. If a thought arises, you must immediately stop it so that you can keep your stillness. Then get rid of all illusions, desires, and wandering thoughts. Needless to say, you must maintain this stillness day and night. Extinguish the active mind but keep the reflective mind. Focus the empty mind but do not let it become static. Do not get stuck in one routine but always keep the mind still.

It is difficult for beginning practitioners to stop thinking. If you cannot extinguish your thoughts, you should stop meditating before you make mistakes. Otherwise, thoughts rising and falling will battle each other and send ripples of repercussion through your body.

With time, your practice will stabilize. When not one thought arises, you will erase the karma of a thousand lifetimes. When you attain stillness in your meditation, you should carry this state of mind to everyday activities such as walking, standing, sitting, and sleeping. In the midst of events and excitement, be relaxed and composed. Whether things are happening or not, your mind should be empty. It should be as if it does not exist. You should hold on to stillness and softness and not let the inner direction be distracted from oneness.

If you are impatient and want to rush things along, you will eventually become ill. Your temper will explode and you will be crazy. This is why you should be patient. Your mind should be still but relaxed. Do not hurry. Let everything go according to its pace. If you can control your thoughts so that nothing will arise, if you can let go and not let the mind wander, and if you can be relaxed and not be bothered by things in the world, you will have no worries. This is true stillness. If things work against you, you will not be frustrated. If you are buffeted by great forces, you will remain relaxed. Use nonaction as the true dwelling and action as response. All forms should be like reflections on the surface of a polished mirror. Let compassion guide your ways, and you will enter stillness.

It is not up to human effort to determine whether enlightenment will come soon or late. Keep your stillness and do not be impatient for enlightenment. Impatience injures original nature, and when you are injured, enlightenment cannot occur. When you are still and do not force things to happen, enlightenment will come naturally. This is true enlightenment.

It is folly if you attain enlightenment and do not make

use of it. If you can keep your stillness in enlightenment, this is doubly wonderful. If in stillness thoughts arise and monsters come to tempt you, let your mind deal with them naturally. If you see a host of celestial lords and immortals, you are seeing the images of your true form.

Let no thoughts arise from the beginning. This is called being open and not looking back. Let no thoughts arise at the end. This is called not having a past. Let the old habits diminish and do not accumulate new ones. Let nothing contaminate or obstruct you. Shed the dust and throw off the cage. Practice this long enough, and you will naturally attain the Tao.

Those who attain the Tao go through seven stages. First, the mind will become still easily and the dust of the world will not cling to the senses. Second, the hundred illnesses are kept at bay and mind and body are light and fresh. Third, depleted energy is restored and lost years are recovered. Fourth, the life span is increased and the practitioner becomes an immortal. Fifth, the body is transformed into vapor and the individual becomes a completely realized being. Sixth, vapor is transformed into spirit and the individual becomes a spirit being. Seventh, the spirit merges with the Tao and the practitioner becomes a being above all beings.

With continued practice, inner strength develops, and the light within will become bright. When the Tao is fully realized, original nature will be round and complete. If you practice this for a long time, the body will be at one with itself, all impurities will be purged, all forms will become nothingness, and original nature will emerge. This is called realizing the Tao. The principle of seeking the Tao is nothing but this.

Thoughts arise from the stirring of images. Fire emerges from attachment. These all disturb original nature. When this happens, we lose our connection with the Origin, the Tao. Know that stopping the mind stops desire. Understand that stirrings in the mind create worries. If you know that the mind is originally empty, you will know the gate to all mysteries.

**Seven Taoist Masters**

This excerpt illustrates the style of meditation practiced by the northern branch of the Complete Reality school, specifically the Lung-men sect. This branch of the Complete Reality school focuses on cultivating mind before body.

It is said that of all the Taoist sects, the northern branch of the Complete Reality school is most similar to Zen Buddhism. In the following excerpt, you will notice that like Zen meditation, Northern Complete Reality meditation requires the practitioner to empty the mind of thoughts. Furthermore, like Zen meditation, there are no visual or auditory aids.

However, the form of meditation practiced by the Complete Reality school is not identical to Zen meditation. Compete Reality Taoism is an internal-alchemical school, and its practice is designed to cultivate both body and mind. When you read the following excerpt, notice the details of posture and the use of *ch'i-kung* techniques, such as knocking the teeth together and swallowing saliva, in this form of meditation.

## *From* Seven Taoist Masters, *Chapter 8*

Ma Tan-yang and Sun Pu-erh asked about meditation. Wang Ch'ung-yang said, "In meditation all thoughts must cease. When the ego is dead, the spirit emerges. When you sit, sit on a cushion. Loosen your clothing. At the hour of tzu (11:00 P.M.), cross your legs gently and sit facing east. Clasp your hands together and place them in front of your body. Your back should be straight. Strike your teeth together and swallow your saliva. Place the tongue against the palate of your mouth. You should be alert in listening, but do not be attached to sounds. Let your eyes drop, but do not close them. Focus on the light that you see in front of you and concentrate on the lower *tan-t'ien*. In meditation it is very important to stop thinking. If thoughts arise, the spirit will not be pure, and your efforts of cultivation will come to nothing. In addition, you should drop all feelings. Once feelings arise, the heart will not be still, and the attainment of the Tao is impossible."

Wang Ch'ung-yang continued, "Sit on a cushion and you will be able to sit long and not feel tired. Loosen your clothing so the movement of internal energy will not be constricted. The hour of tzu is when the first ray of yang appears. Face east because the breath of life flows in from the east at the hour of the first yang. Clasp your hands in the *t'ai-chi* symbol, because it symbolizes emptiness of form. Sit with your back straight, because only with a vertical spine can the energy rise to the head. Close your mouth and place the tongue against the palate so that the internal energy cannot dissipate. The ear is associated with generative energy. Being attached to sound will dissipate this energy. Do not close your eyes, for they let the light in to shine on your spirit. If you close your eyes, the spirit will be dimmed. If you open them too wide, the spirit will escape. Therefore you should lower the lids but not close them. Concentrate on the lower *tan-t'ien* as if to reflect the light of your eyes onto it because here is the mystery of all things. Minimize speech, as this conserves vital energy. Rest your ears, as this conserves generative energy. Dissolve thoughts to conserve spirit energy. When all these energies are not dissipated, then you will attain immortality."

# 10

## *The Arts of Longevity*

### CULTIVATING THE BODY

C ULTIVATING THE BODY IS AN IMPOR-
tant part of Taoist spirituality. Without a healthy
body, enlightenment, or union with the Tao, is not
possible. Moreover, a long and healthy life gives us time to
prepare ourselves to return to the Tao when we leave the
mortal realm.

The readings in this chapter present some prominent
Taoist techniques of cultivating the body and improving
physical health. Please do not use them as manuals. Unguided practice of these techniques can be harmful, and
the author and publisher are not responsible for any complications that result from using these readings as manuals.

### Yi-men ch'ang-seng pi-shu
### (*Chen Hsi-yi's Secret Methods of Longevity*)

The *Yi-men ch'ang-seng pi-shu* is a collection of techniques
practiced by the Taoist sects of Hua-shan. These sects all
claim the Sung-dynasty (960–1279 CE) hermit Chen Hsi-

yi as their patriarch. *Yi-men* means the "School of Hsi-yi." Compiled during the Wan-li (1573–1619 CE) years of the Ming dynasty by a Taoist hermit named Chou Fu-ching, the book postdated both the Cheng-t'ung and Wan-li Taoist canons. However, it is included in Hsiao T'ien-shih's *Tao-tsang ching-hua* (The Essential Works of the Taoist Canon), a contemporary collection of canonical and postcanonical Taoist scriptures.

In the *Yi-men ch'ang-seng pi-shu* are descriptions of ch'i-kung postures, Taoist calisthenics, massage, breath-control techniques, and meditation. Of all the texts collected in the book, the *Chih-feng sui* (Red Phoenix Calisthenics) is the most famous. Reputed to be transmitted by Chen Hsi-yi himself, the book is profusely illustrated. It describes sitting, standing, and sleeping ch'i-kung postures, calisthenics, and techniques for control and regulation of the breath.

The illustrations that follow are from the *Chih-feng sui*. They depict techniques of massage, Taoist calisthenics, breath control and regulation, and sleeping ch'i-kung. Accompanying each picture is a description of the method and the health benefits.

左右單轆轤三
十六次

*Massage and kneading techniques from the* Chi-feng sui (Red
Phoenix Calisthenics). "Roll the knuckles over the areas left
and right of the gate [Life Gate] thirty-six times.

兩手摩腎堂三十六次以數多更妙

*Massage and kneading techniques from the* Chi-feng sui. *"Using both hands, rub and apply pressure to the area around the kidneys thirty-six times. The more this is repeated, the better the effect."*

叩齒集神三
十六次双手
抱崑崙双手
擊天鼓二十
四次

*Massage and kneading techniques from the* Chi-feng sui. *"Knock the teeth together thirty-six times to gather the spirit. Take both hands and hold the* kun-lun *(spine). Hit the Heavenly Drum twenty-four times." The Heavenly Drum is the flat part of the skull on two sides of the Jade Pillow cavity, where the spine enters the skull.*

兩手相搓當呵五呵後义
手托天按頂各九次

*Taoist calisthenics from the* Chi-feng sui. *"Position both arms in front of the chest. Expel air five times. Then stretch the arms upward above the head. Repeat this cycle nine times."*

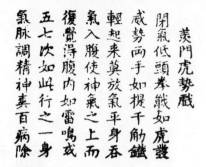

羨門虎勢戲
閉氣低頭拳戰如虎勢
咸勢兩手如撼千觔鐵
輕起來莫放氣平身吞
氣入腹使神氣之上而
復覺得腹內如雷鳴或
五七次如此行之一身
氣脈調精神奕百病除

*Techniques of regulating and directing breath from the* Chi-feng
sui: *the Tiger Posture of Hsin-men.* "Stop the breath, lower the
head, and hold the fists like a tiger ready to strike. The arms
should be powerful as if they are lifting a thousand catties
[a Chinese measurement of weight]. Gradually straighten up. Do
not let the breath out but swallow it back when you have
straightened. The breath enters the belly to let the energy of the
spirit rise. The belly should feel like thunder rumbling. Do this
five or seven times. The energy in the meridians will be regulated,
the spirit will be clear, and a hundred illnesses will leave."

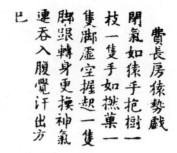

巴 連 脚 隻 枝 閉 費
　 吞 跟 脚 一 氣 長
　 入 轉 虛 隻 如 房
　 腹 身 空 手 猿 猿
　 覺 更 握 如 手 勢
　 汗 撲 趄 撚 抱 戲
　 出 神 一 菓 樹
　 方 氣 隻 一 一

*Techniques of regulating and directing breath from the* Chi-feng
sui: *the Ape Posture of Fei Ch'ang-fang. "Stop the breath and
hold your hands like an ape hanging from a tree. Then close the
fingers of one hand to imitate an ape picking a fruit. Shift the
weight completely off one leg. Turn the body around and gather
the energy of the spirit. Swallow deep into the belly until
perspiration appears."*

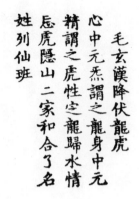

*Sleeping ch'i-kung postures from the* Chi-feng sui: *Mao Hsüan-han's Posture of Subduing and Overcoming the Dragon and Tiger. "The original vapor in the heart is known as the body of the dragon. The generative energy in the circle of the middle is called the original nature of the tiger. When the dragon returns to the water, emotions are dissolved, and the tiger hides in the mountain. The two families are in harmony, and your name will be listed among the immortals."*

麻衣真人和調真炁
調和真炁五朝元心息相
依念不偏二物長居於戊
巳虎龍盤結大丹圓

*Sleeping ch'i-kung postures from the* Chi-feng sui: *Enlightened Being Mah-i's Method of Regulating the True Vapor. "Regulate the true vapor and the five breaths will return to the origin. The mind is at rest and thoughts are not wayward. The two substances [mind and life] dwell forever in the positions of* wu *and* ssu *[the yin and yang in the center of the heart]. The tiger and the dragon copulate to produce the great round pill."*

## Chang San-feng t'ai-chi lien-tan pi-chüeh
*(Chang San-feng's Secret T'ai-chi Method for Cultivating the Elixir)*

Chang San-feng is best known as the patriarch of the Wu-tang-shan sect and the originator of *t'ai-chi ch'uan,* an exercise for cultivating health and longevity. T'ai-chi ch'uan is also considered to be an internal martial art, because while cultivating body and mind, practitioners can also develop self-defense skills.

It is said that Chang San-feng originally devised a set of thirteen movements, which was later expanded to one hundred and eight by his students. Therefore, in the literature of t'ai-chi ch'uan we find many references to the Thirteen Postures, although the complete t'ai-chi set today consists of one hundred and eight moves.

For Chang San-feng, t'ai-chi ch'uan is not to be confused with t'ai-chi. While the *ch'uan* is a set of movements, t'ai-chi is a state of spiritual development. Thus, the movements of t'ai-chi ch'uan are a means to attain the state of t'ai-chi, which is the balance of the yin and yang energies in the body.

Chang San-feng wrote several treatises on t'ai-chi ch'uan, ch'i-kung, and meditation. These texts and his students' commentaries are collected in a book titled *Chang San-feng t'ai-chi lien-tan pi-chüeh* (Chang San-feng's Secret T'ai-chi Method for Cultivating the Elixir). This text is not listed in the Ming dynasty Taoist canons, but it is published in the series of Taoist texts edited by Taoist scholar Hsiao

T'ien-shih of Taiwan. It appears as volume 5, part 2, in the *Tao-tsang ching-hua* (The Essential Works of the Taoist Canon).

The following excerpts are chosen to illustrate how t'ai-chi ch'uan, an internal martial art, can be used to cultivate physical health and mental clarity.

## Understanding the Work of the Thirteen Postures

Use the mind to move the ch'i to let it sink. Then the ch'i can be absorbed into the bones. Use ch'i to move the body, letting it happen naturally. Then ch'i will follow the mind with ease. Let the spirit be directed upward, and nothing will feel cumbersome.

What is meant by being suspended by the top of the head? It means that intention and ch'i should be lively and movement should be agile, rounded, and light. What is meant by alternating the substantial and insubstantial? It means that each movement should be grounded in relaxation and stillness and fully directed toward one point.

When you stand, the body should be balanced and comfortable. The feet and arms should be ready to respond to the eight directions. Move the ch'i like a pearl circulating nine times. The energy should flow in the body without obstruction. The movement should be as strong as steel tempered a hundred times. The foundation should be impregnable. Move with the stealth of a ghost. Be focused like a cat stalking a mouse. Be still like a great mountain.

Move like a flowing river. Hold your force like a pulled bow. Let the force out like a speeding arrow. In its indirect path maintain straightness. Hold your force and only let it out after the opponent has made his move.

Force should come from the spine. The feet should move according to the body's movement. Let go and then hold on. Coming and going should be like a cascade. Alternate advance and retreat. Only in softness can you be firm. Only when you can breathe can your movement be agile.

Cultivate the ch'i and let it rise. Then there will be no problems. Let the force be indirect and hidden, and there will be plenty to spare. Let the mind be the commander. Let the ch'i be the herald. Let the spine be the pivot. In the beginning, aim to expand. Later, aim to contract. Then you can hide your action.

Thus, it is said, "Start first with the mind. Then follow with the body." Relax the abdomen. Draw the ch'i into the bones. Calm the spirit and still the body. Let this be planted in your mind. In every movement there is stillness, and in every stillness there is movement. Moving forward and backward, let the ch'i run along your back, drawing it into the spinal column. Internally, the spirit is stable. Externally, the composure is leisurely. Walk like a cat. Move like pulling silk. Focus and attention are in the spirit, not in the breath. If it is in the breath, there will be problems. If there is effortful breathing there is no strength. However, when there is no breathing, the breath is pure and strong. Then the ch'i will be like a wheel and the spine will be like the axle.

## Ten Important Things to Do in Your Practice

1. Clean the face regularly.
2. Rub the eyes regularly.
3. Flick the ears regularly.
4. Knock the teeth together regularly.
5. Always keep the back warm.
6. Always protect the chest.
7. Massage the abdomen regularly.
8. Rub the feet together regularly.
9. Swallow the saliva regularly.
10. Always maintain flexibility in the waist and spine.

## Ten Things to Avoid in Your Practice

1. Getting up too early.
2. Getting chilled in a shady room.
3. Sitting on wet ground.
4. Getting chilled in wet clothes.
5. Becoming too hot.
6. Perspiring in a breeze.
7. Sleeping with lights on.
8. Having sexual intercourse at the hour of *tzu* (11:00 P.M. to 1:00 A.M.).
9. Immersing muscles and tendons in cold water.
10. Putting hot food in the stomach.

## Eighteen Injuries to Be Avoided

1. Watch too long and the generative energy will be damaged.
2. Listen too long and the spirit will be damaged.
3. Lie down too long and the vital energy (ch'i) will be damaged.
4. Sit too long and the meridians will be harmed.
5. Stand too long and the bones will be damaged.
6. Walk too much and the tendons will be damaged.
7. Anger harms the liver.
8. Scheming harms the spleen.
9. Worrying harms the heart.
10. Excessive sadness harms the lungs.
11. Overeating harms the stomach.
12. Excessive fear harms the kidneys.
13. Too much laughter harms the abdomen.
14. Too much talking harms the spinal fluid.
15. Sleep too much and the saliva will be damaged.
16. Perspire too much and the yang energy will be harmed.
17. Cry too often and the blood will be harmed.
18. Too much sex will harm the marrow.